EXHIBITIONS

Essays on Art and Atrocity

EXHIBITIONS

Jehanne Dubrow

University of New Mexico Press | Albuquerque

ISBN 978-0-8263-6526-2 (paper)
ISBN 978-0-8263-6527-9 (electronic)

Library of Congress Cataloging-in-Publication data is on file with the Library of Congress

Founded in 1889, the University of New Mexico sits on the traditional homelands of the
Pueblo of Sandia. The original peoples of New Mexico—Pueblo, Navajo, and Apache—
since time immemorial have deep connections to the land and have made significant
contributions to the broader community statewide. We honor the land itself and those who
remain stewards of this land throughout the generations and also acknowledge our committed relationship to Indigenous peoples. We gratefully recognize our history.

Book epigraph used with permission of Beacon Press, from *Still Life with Oysters and Lemon:
On Objects and Intimacy* by Mark Doty, © 2002; permission conveyed through Copyright
Clearance Center, Inc.

Cover photograph: courtesy of Annie Spratt on Unsplash
Designed by Felicia Cedillos
Composed in Adobe Garamiond Pro

For my parents,
who taught me the beauty and terror of looking at the world.

All those painters, all their lives looking at reality with such scrupulous attention, attention pouring out and out, and what does it give us back but ourselves?

—Mark Doty
Still Life with Oysters and Lemon

Contents

GALLERY FOUR

GALLERY FIVE

GALLERY SIX

GALLERY ONE

Landscape with Basilica

I was born in the city of Palladio. Palazzi and palazzi. The creamy skin of stucco over brick. Landscape an illusion painted on a wall.

I was poisoned into life, my mother sickened on bad cheese, its surface like blue-veined marble. Later they would call me Little Gorgon—delivered as if from the underworld, my mouth molded into shrieking, the wispy snakes of hair around my head.

The doctor told my mother to walk the fields, "to bring the baby out," he said. She pushed across the grass for hours, keeping the hospital always in her view.

I was born on a day of remembering. In some countries, they wore poppies in lapels. In some, they laid a flag beside a tomb.

I was born in time for dinner. "Always ready to devour," my father said. He took the stone streets alone, and a café opened to let him in. There was pizza and pizza. There were salad leaves glazed with oil. There were ruby goblets lifted to the light.

GALLERY TWO

The Red Picture and the Blue

According to the story, my third word—after "Mommy" and "Daddy"—was "picture." In Zagreb, where I spent the first two years of my life, my mother lifted me from my pram to see the pieces of art. "Look. Look at the picture." On sunny days, we took the funicular from our apartment in the old section of the city downhill to the lower, newer portion, where we visited galleries or just toured the neighborhoods. Or we wandered closer to home through cobblestone streets to St. Mark's Church—with its ecstasy of colorful roof tiles—only a few blocks away. Even if we stayed indoors, we could gaze down from the windows of our apartment into the courtyard of the Meštrović Atelier, a gallery dedicated to one of Yugoslavia's most renowned artists. The rumor went that, years before, Meštrović himself had slept in the very rooms where we now slept, had eaten where we now ate, had regarded the same medieval views of Zagreb. Our dining room, which was punctuated with a series of rounded alcoves, once displayed the sculptor's works-in-progress.

And so I kept saying "picturepicturepicture." I stretched my hand toward the beautiful. In my first year, laid on the living room floor, I pulled lint from the wool rug, rolling the soft balls of color between my finger and thumb. My mother swears she used to find me arranging these kernels of bright lint in intricate patterns, placing small nubs of orange beside specks of yellow and green. I could stay like this for hours, my liquid infant gaze focused on the swirl of design and hue. Already I saw the flowers woven in the carpet and made my own in turn.

It was the mid-1970s, my parents' first post. Before my birth, they spent a little over a year in Belgrade, after which they moved to Zagreb, where my father was the Deputy Cultural Affairs Officer. At the US Cultural Center, the Foreign Service Nationals (or FSNs, as they're known), called me "sweetica," the English word paired with the affectionate Serbo-Croatian diminutive "-ica." Little sweetie. I was so tiny my father could fit my head in his palm, my feet barely reaching the crook of his arm.

At the end of four years in Yugoslavia, less than a week before we were about to leave for our next assignment—this time in Zaire—my parents received a phone call. Good news: Mersad Berber, the great Bosnian Muslim painter, had agreed to sell my parents something. The artist didn't often accept American patronage. Apparently, an American tourist, upon entering his studio, had once asked with dismay, "Is this the only stuff you do?" But Berber had been persuaded, at last, that my parents were sincere in their admiration, and he decided to let them have two paintings.

When I was old enough to categorize such things, I came to think of them as the red painting and the blue. In the first, the rectangular canvas is divided perfectly in half. A woman watches from the top portion. Her long neck is visible, her elaborate headdress dotted with speckles of gold. What at first appears to be a curved shadow behind her is, in fact, the dark torso of a horse, its head bending toward the white horse who stares up from the bottom of the painting, its eyes rolled back in its head as if in fear or agitation. And leaking through both woman and animals is a ruby backdrop that charges the whole painting with an alarmed and pulsing beauty.

By contrast, the blue painting is a site of serenity. At the bottom of the canvas: the top half of a woman. The shape of her headdress mirrors the city behind her, a skyline of narrow turrets and onion domes. The ever blue of the sky is streaked with gilding, its metallic shimmer like a constant nightfall.

Later, I would understand that in these women I saw the visual echoes of religious icons. There was something both ornate and plain about the paintings. The women were luminous, holy, their faces round like porcelain bowls glimmering with hand-applied gold leaf, their pointed chins perching on the tall, formed stems of their necks, the continuous, slender lines of eyebrow joined to nose joined to eyebrow, and the delicate dots of their mouths. The artist treats the women with tenderness, his brush respectful against their features.

Throughout my childhood, the two women watched me like a pair of tranquil guardians from their elevated positions on the wall of the dining room. They were there through hundreds of evening meals, the many afternoons I did my homework at the long table that seated eight. In college, when I read Plato's *Phaedrus* for the first time, I thought about the two horses in the red painting, the pale one rearing back, attempting to escape the frame, and the other a muscular shadow, leaning over to nip the neck of its companion. "In the case of the human soul," Plato writes, "first of all, it is a pair of horses that the charioteer dominates; one of them is noble and handsome and of good breeding, while the other is the very opposite, so that our charioteer necessarily has a difficult and troublesome task."

Throughout my childhood, too, we lived in places that might have been called divided. Consider the linguistic discord of Belgium, the international push-pull over Zaire's natural resources, and Poland, which so often, throughout its history, was merely territory to be invaded by the armies of its powerful neighbors. But no country seemed more divided than Yugoslavia, its soul dragged in opposing directions, like a chariot pulled by a pair of antagonistic horses.

My parents speak about how much they loved their time in Belgrade and Zagreb. They remember the roasted meats, the assertive green of the olive oils, the sturdy, rough table wines. "The people were so warm," they tell me. But, my mother says, it was unwise to mention the Croats to the Serbs or the Serbs to the Croats. Then, she explains, the response was always, "those terrible, terrible people." Most Americans can't understand this kind of long historical memory, both sides talking about battles that occurred eight hundred years before, as if the wars had happened yesterday.

For nearly forty years, until his death in 1980, the dictator known as Tito governed Yugoslavia, a nation-state composed of six distinct socialist republics: Bosnia and Herzegovina, Croatia, Macedonia, Montenegro, Serbia, and Slovenia. Named president for life in 1974, Tito kept strict control of the country and tamped down ancient ethnic conflicts. By the fall of the Berlin Wall in 1989, Yugoslavia was moving toward dissolution, Communist rule no longer a restraint on old, well-tended hatreds. As journalist Dusko Doder puts it,

> Ever since Emperor Constantine decided to split the Roman Empire in the fourth century A.D., the tectonic plates of imperial, religious, and racial interests have ground together in the Balkans. Rome and Constantinople, Catholicism and Orthodoxy, Christianity and Islam, Germans and Slavs, Russia and the West—all have clashed along a shifting fault line running down the middle of the former Yugoslavia.

Like strata of soil, successive enmities—such as the "cycle of unrest and violence" of Hapsburg rule, of WWI, and then of WWII—were layered over earlier grudges and resentments. By the late 1980s, Doder explains, "Serbian communist strongman Slobodan Milošević rode to power . . . on the crest of a powerful nationalist wave," and "nationalist parties were swept into power in all republics in the first free post-Cold War elections in 1990."

What followed the rise of nationalism in the former Yugoslavia were wars in Croatia, Bosnia and Herzegovina, and Kosovo, as well as conflicts in Macedonia and the Preševo Valley. The worst of the violence was called "ethnic cleansing," a term that ensured the United States and other nations could avoid the kind of intervention that might have been necessitated by labeling the crimes genocide.

By 1993, when the war was already well underway in Yugoslavia, we were posted to Brussels. One night, my mother told us that, in addition to the bombings, the sieges of towns, the mass disappearances of civilians, there were now rumors of rapes emerging from the territories of the former Yugoslavia. No, there were rumors of rape camps. And my mother, with her excellent language skills and her knowledge of the region, had been identified as a suitable representative to fly to Zagreb and to interview Bosnian refugees.

In an unpublished essay she once wrote for a creative writing workshop, my mother recounts how she felt at the time: "When I received a message from a former State Department colleague that my name had come up on the language database as possible team leader, I had shoved the cable aside and tried to ignore it." Over dinner, we discussed if my mother should take the assignment. "I don't want to go," my mother said. My father stayed silent. And, although I have no memory of this conversation, my mother writes that I told her, "Mommy, if you don't go, somebody else will have to. And what if that person doesn't believe the women?"

Believe the women. I would have been barely seventeen when I said this. In her essay, my mother hypothesizes that I knew women could be disbelieved because I had heard her own story from thirty years before. When she was nineteen and living in Miami, my mother was held hostage by a man who had escaped from an institution, the kind of place that used to be called an asylum for the criminally insane. For nearly a day, he held her at knifepoint in her own apartment, saying over and over, "Tell me a story. Tell me why I shouldn't kill you."

My mother obeyed. She told him about the college classes she was taking. She pointed to the textbooks that lay open on the dining room table. She bandaged the man's hand, which she had cut in the struggle, after he broke into her rooms.

"Tell me a story," he said. "Tell me why I shouldn't kill you."

She offered to cook him dinner. Spaghetti and meatballs, she suggested, knowing she didn't have those ingredients in her kitchen, that they would have to walk to the grocery store and that the store stood across the street from a police station. She took a purse from the closet; its sides were sturdy, the bottom studded with four metal feet. She placed her shopping list inside the bag. And when my mother finally managed to get away from the man— knocking him over with a sudden strike of the purse—she ran and ran.

In the police station, her face and neck and wrists still bruised from his fingers, the officers on duty didn't believe the story she told. Women like this were always coming in to complain about their boyfriends' fists.

"Go home," they told her. "Just tell him you're sorry and won't do it again."

And this is why my mother decided to go to Yugoslavia: to listen to the women.

There had been shelling in the suburbs outside of Zagreb, but the war was mostly felt in other ways within the city. Refugees were everywhere. And hyperinflation rapidly changed the price of a cup of coffee or a loaf of bread from one day to the next.

It was cold in Zagreb. My mother had packed thermal underwear, sweaters, a thick scarf to wear indoors if the power flickered out. On some days, she and the rest of the team interviewed women in the offices of NGOs or in the makeshift spaces of refugee camps. They went to hospitals, often sitting with women in the psychiatric wings. Depending on a woman's health—how hurt her body, how abraded her speech—an interview might last four, six, even eight hours. Or the conversation would become too difficult, and my mother would sit quietly in a nearby chair, while nurses or doctors shuffled through the corridors beyond.

And although my mother, a gifted linguist, spoke Serbo-Croatian, she brought a translator with her to each interview, the pace of the conversation halting and stumbling as questions and answers were mediated through translation. My mother wanted it this way. She wanted to construct a small, artificial barrier of language, so that the women's trauma might take longer to reach her: "I was quite certain that the stories I would hear would be devastating. I needed to make sure that my emotions did not interfere with getting the facts."

Interviews began with slow, careful introductions. This is who we are. We understand you might have a story. We are interested in hearing your story, but only if you feel comfortable talking to us. Tell us about your life before the war. Tell us about your town. Did you know your neighbors?

And, later on in the conversation: Did you know any of your captors? Do you remember a name? How were the women and girls separated from the men? Where were you taken?

The work of the team was to collect testimony for the UN's War Tribunal. Patterns of abuse—pointing to the systematic use of rape as part of the Serbs' genocidal practices against their Bosnian neighbors—needed to emerge carefully from the interviews. The questions could not lead, could not force an answer, must be able to stand up to scrutiny in an international court of law.

My mother stayed in Zagreb approximately six weeks. Each night, when the interviews were done, she came back to the hotel to work on her notes. The embassy had given her a secure typewriter; after she transcribed each interview, she locked the pages and the typewriter ribbon in the safe in her room. My mother has never been a drinker. Instead, she took a long shower, trying to wash the words from her skin. She went to bed, although she seldom fell asleep easily. She hadn't been raped by the man who held her hostage decades before, but my mother couldn't help remembering her own story when she heard the Bosnian women recounting theirs: his hands around her neck, how he kept saying, "Tell me why I shouldn't kill you."

And once she returned to Brussels, my mother spoke "incessantly," as she recalls it, about the interviews. Each night, she sat at the dinner table, the rest of us listening, never interrupting the tumble of her words, as she recounted more details of her weeks in Zagreb, perhaps the lacerated face of a victim she met in the hospital or the dried-leaf tremble of a voice.

I often wonder if my mother chose to go back to Zagreb in 1993, in part, because she was seeing, up close, in the daily cables and other communications from Washington, DC, that the United States would not intercede to stop the fighting. Academic and diplomat Samantha Power writes in her Pulitzer Prize–winning book *"A Problem from Hell": America and the Age of Genocide*:

> Before I began exploring America's relationship with genocide, I used to refer to U.S. policy toward Bosnia as a "failure." I have changed my mind. It is daunting to acknowledge, but this country's consistent policy of nonintervention in the face of genocide offers sad testimony not to a broken American political system but to one that is ruthlessly effective. The system, as it stands now, is *working*. No U.S. president has ever made genocide prevention a priority, and no U.S. president has ever suffered politically for his indifference to its occurrence. It is thus no coincidence that genocide rages on.

There were plenty of reasons for political inaction. Power explains that "the

U.S. military advised against it," the Clinton administration "would act only with the consent and active participation of their European partners," and the president "was worried about American public opinion." The violence continued. And, according to the United Nations International Criminal Tribunal for the former Yugoslavia, in Bosnia and Herzegovina alone it was "estimated that more than 100,000 people were killed and two million people, more than half the population, were forced to flee their homes as a result of the war that raged from April 1992 through to November 1995 . . . Thousands of Bosnian women were systematically raped. Notorious detention centres for civilians were set up by all conflicting sides."

In 1992, Mersad Berber—like many Bosniaks (Bosnian Muslims)—was forced to flee his home. Both during the Balkan Wars and after, until his death in 2012, the artist produced paintings that could be said to function as a form of witness, as testimony, or as visual representations of the region's trauma. He created ambitious sequences such as *Dubrovnik War Diary*, *Sarajevo War Diary—Midnight Talks with Il Guercino*, and later *The Great Allegory of Srebrenica*. Art historian Aida Abadžić Hodžić writes that Berber "tried to find a human face in this vortex of what was often a brutal history, to reach out to the Other and to show the multi-layered and turbulent history of Bosnia and Herzegovina." His pieces combine collage, drawing, painting, and digital printing and, as art critic Edward Lucie-Smith says, "do not deal with single images but with conjunctions of images, in some cases simply placed side by side, but in others layered one on top of the other. In this way they often seem to mirror some of the complexities of Balkan culture and history."

I study a painting from a 2015 exhibition catalogue. *Great Allegory on Srebrenica VIII* (2005) is described as mixed media on paper. Against a background of torn pages of books, old photographs, and rough splotches like crumbling plaster on a building, Berber has painted the anguished head and torso of a man, who could be dying or already dead, his eyes fixed on something we can't see. The man is painted in the style of Velázquez, one of Berber's great influences, his body touched with a chilly moonlight, shadows darkening behind him. He is surrounded by blocks of red paint the color of dried blood. A group of armless hands float near him, too large in proportion to the scale of his form, as if he has been laid among the remnants of classical statues, his limbs blending with the marble miscellanies. And near the top right corner is a horse's head, sepia-stained and still, so different from the horses in the red painting of my childhood.

Abadžić Hodžić calls the horse the "central metaphor of most of Berber's cycles" and points out that "it was not, in Berber's words, a grand horse, but the working packhorse of the mountains of Bosnia, so deeply linked to all paths of life: hard labour and weddings, funerals and wars. That was the horse in whose expressive power, pain and imperfect beauty one may read the biography of his people." To be a divided country is not to be a land always at war with itself. There are many horses. Sometimes the horse pulls a wagon full of hay. Or it is adorned with bright ribbons in honor of a neighbor's wedding. Perhaps it is hitched to a cart that carries the body of someone beloved by the village. And only occasionally is it used to escape the fighting or to charge at the terror.

Berber made *Great Allegory on Srebrenica VIII* ten years after the massacre in that city, during which more than eight thousand Bosnian Muslim men and boys were murdered by Bosnian Serbs. About Berber's paintings of Srebrenica, Lucie-Smith writes that "[t]he images are a lament, not only for those who died, but for the demise of the plural culture that flourished, despite all ethnic and religious antagonisms, for some hundreds of years in the Balkans." I look at the pieces Berber created in the last decade of his life and can see how paper and paint are placed on top of one another, sometimes obscuring what's underneath, sometimes revealing unsettling intersections of media.

A few years ago, I read an advertisement in the local online classifieds. For a hundred dollars, someone was selling a limited-edition archival print by Mersad Berber. My husband and I drove to the woman's house in the suburbs. She came out, carrying the piece in its bulky, wooden frame, large enough that she struggled to lift it with both hands. When she turned the glass to face me, I gasped. It was a reproduction of the blue painting, signed by the artist, with hand-applied gilding around the edges. There she was again: the woman, serene and staring, a skyline of bartizans and rounded roofs behind her.

I had always preferred the fearful drama of the red painting, the two horses challenging one another with their bright, unblinking eyes. Art is about tension, I so often tell my creative writing students. I loved the red painting because it was entirely tense, bared teeth and tightened muscles. But the blue painting—or, at least, this reproduction—would have to do. I would hang it in my hallway, so that I might pass the woman every day, her eyes always on me and mine on hers.

And, maybe, it is better to have this blue-gray tranquility instead of so much red. Maybe it's better to live without the multiplicity of the horses and their "expressive power."

It now seems impossible that the former Yugoslavia was ever a landscape untouched by hurt, just as it is hard to imagine my mother was ever unafraid of blacked-out rooms, not frightened by the wind that jostles the door handle like someone trying to get inside. Even today, she does not enter a darkened space. Instead, she reaches a hand around the corner, feeling for the light switch.

As for all the women she interviewed, what happened to them? My mother doesn't know. She doesn't even know what happened to her own interview reports once they were transmitted to the International Criminal Tribunal in The Hague. The testimonies she collected probably joined hundreds of others, some of which were eventually used in the Tribunal's court cases. But she is certain her reports did "add to the corpus of evidence that had been gathered from numerous sources, proving that war crimes had been committed." I hope this comforts her. We both know that many of the women continue to crouch within the shadows of their rapists, who may live in nearby villages, only a few kilometers away. Intimate partner violence is common, too. And the children born out of wartime rape are sometimes despised for their parentage or flattened into symbols of nationalism, heroic sacrifice.

Today, I call my mother. I ask how well she remembers the women she met in Zagreb twenty-seven years ago. She says that many of them blur together.

"Their stories were so alike," she says.

But there is one whose voice my mother can hear. The woman had been raped and then, in the camp, was forced to take care of a young girl who had been assaulted, too, to wash her face or force bites of food into her mouth, to keep her alive so that the child "could continue to be raped." One day, the girl was taken away, and the woman never saw her again.

"She had her own grief and then the additional grief that she had somehow failed. She lived with these two terrible things." My mother goes quiet on the other end of the line. I am quiet too. For a minute, we sit together, listening to one another's breathing.

"Look," my mother used to say when I was a baby. "Look at the picture." As Berber's decades of art demonstrate, it isn't simple work to stare directly at trauma. On the canvas, trauma resists retelling. Like the women's stories my mother once transcribed, trauma itself is a thing of fragmentation, of disjointed time. It tears at the edges. It needs gluing together. It needs painting over or scraping away. To approach trauma, the artist must engage in an act of translation, moving obliquely, toward a still room where a figure waits, preparing to speak.

Snapshot / Warsaw, 1981

[Perched between bedtime and awake, I sat on the staircase. In the rooms above, there were curtains barely closed on a field of December, the ground prickled bare. Through the spindles, I looked to the room below, the world suddenly cut into strips of vision. My father kept answering the phone. "Słucham," *I'm listening*, he said. My mother had turned on the lights, and in the yellow brightness I could see someone had dropped the tiny spear of a toothpick, its point angled in the carpet. The guests—people who taught or told stories, who sent news across the border—could not go home. Men in uniform would be waiting to take them. Someone said "curfew." Someone laughed in a way that sounded like gasping. On the wall, the clock hands were flinching their nervous time.]

The Dead Class

Tadeusz Kantor is already dead in the small self-portrait, his jaw held shut with a cloth that loops under the chin and ties at the top of his head. Scratch marks outline his clavicle. The skull is drawn as well, in both senses of the word. What pain the body felt at the end remains apparent here, shoulders lifting toward the ears, the mouth a tight knot. A thumb-tip has smudged in shadows of cheekbone, hollows around the nose. The artist has imagined his own death mask, has cast his features in bleak repose.

Seeing the piece for the first time, I ask my father, "Why is he wearing a scarf?" I think the man must have a toothache.

"He's dead," my father tells me. I look again—*is this the face of death?* I don't know what to make of the fabric tethered to the paper-white skin.

Approximately the dimensions of a piece of letterhead, the sketch doesn't have the oversized presence of many of the other paintings in my parents' house. Its paper is a sickly tinge. Kantor has used a quick hand to rough out a face and the top of a torso. The whole thing feels urgent, as if the artist is in a race with the death he's depicting. In fact, my parents buy the piece in 1989, less than a year before Kantor dies.

As his obituary in the *New York Times* explains, Tadeusz Kantor was "an internationally known avant-garde theater director, author and painter," one of the great Renaissance men of twentieth-century Polish culture. Born April 6, 1915, in Wielopole, a village in the part of southern Poland that used to be called Galicia, "Kantor was known for creating dynamic, inventive theater based on historical and personal themes," the obituary continues. "He was present in his productions not as an actor but sitting on stage, watching along with the audience."

Watching along with the audience—I understand positioning oneself this way. For many years, I am an only child. And even when, at the age of twelve, I become an older sister, I often remain alone or am left in the care of our housekeeper, Pani Basia. Our home, with its vast spaces for entertaining—a *representational household*, as they say in the Foreign Service—holds several freezers in the basement, enough china and crystal to serve fifty, a great formal table that can be expanded by pulling a lever, an extra leaf sliding into its center. Frequently, I peer around the edges of doors, observing the conversations of grownups. My father is so talented at this kind of performance, his great, low voice projecting across the room, that even from my hidden place, I can hear the charming anecdotes that end with laughter, how easily he shifts from English to Polish to French, a little Italian or German tossed in if the discussion turns to opera.

After a cocktail party, when the guests have left their empty champagne flutes behind, left spoons sitting in glistening gray bowls of caviar, these rooms are quiet. My parents may have already returned to their offices at the US Embassy, long hours of meetings still ahead of them. I sit on a couch, staring at the things on the walls. Sometimes the painted eyes follow mine. Sometimes the mouths seem to curve in a smile. Even the sketch of a corpse can become a companion if I look at him long enough.

⁊

Kantor's most famous and most performed play, *Umarła klasa*, premiered in Kraków in November 1975, four days after my birth. Sometimes described as a "dramatic séance," *The Dead Class* explores what critics characterize as Kantor's central obsessions: the World Wars, Poland's history as a site of invasion and oppressive rule, and the artist's intimate memories of his early life. In 1976, the great Andrzej Wajda—who only a year later would release one of his most renowned films, *Człowiek z marmuru* (*Man of Marble*)—shot the original production of *The Dead Class* as performed by Kantor's theater company, Cricot 2.

In the film, the audience enters the space, which appears to be one of those stone cellars so common in Kraków, the walls carved and ancient, the ceiling and doorway curved. The cast is already there, facing us. Kantor stands, while the rest sit in wooden pews, as if in a classroom or a church. The women wear black dresses, the men black suits, white shirts, black ties, everyone attired for mourning. Each actor raises an arm, pointer and middle finger lifted together. Are they trying to answer a question asked by an invisible teacher? Are they making the Polish sign for victory? Are they waving goodbye? They rise, moving backward and out, silent, silent, until only Kantor and a man still as a puppet—his expression an uncanny mask—remain. Then another man returns to retrieves his strange companion. Then the sound of a waltz. There's dancing with dummies the size of children. Everyone sits again. And finally, someone, an instructor, speaks.

"What do we know about King Solomon?"

එ

Splitting the baby. Polish history is full of partitions and divisions, and later what Holocaust scholar Lawrence Langer terms "choiceless choices."

"What do we know about King Solomon?" the actor asks.

A few minutes later, when the cast begins to chant the first letter of the Hebrew alphabet like a nursery rhyme, "aleph aleph aleph," it becomes clear that *The Dead Class* is concerned not with the dead in general but with the particularities of the Polish dead—which is to say, also Polish Jews, the friends and neighbors Kantor remembered so well from his early years in Wielopole, where more than half of the town's population was once Jewish. "It was a typical eastern small town or *shtetl*," Kantor once said, "with a large market square and a few miserable lanes. In the square stood a chapel, with some sort of saint for the Catholic faithful. In the same square was a well near which Jewish weddings were held, primarily when the moon was full. On one side stood the church, the rectory, and the Catholic cemetery, and on the other the synagogue, the narrow Jewish lanes, and another cemetery, somewhat different."

What do we know about King Solomon?

I am eleven or twelve when I begin to realize that we are Jews. There is almost no religion in our household. So the gradual recognition of our Jewishness has nothing to do with prayers read from a certain book or rules about consuming meat and milk or a parchment scroll affixed to a doorway. Instead, I realize that the party we attend one winter—where all the children receive presents and we eat potato pancakes with apple sauce—is to celebrate not Christmas but Chanukah. There is an earlier memory of a long dinner that included a story of leaving one land for another. A platter holding a bone. Some bitter herbs. We dip our fingers into glasses of wine, tapping red drops on the edge of our plates.

At the American School of Warsaw, my classmates—who come from all over the world—are starting to tell me that I'm a Jew. "Kike," they say, or "Żyd." Sometimes, they indicate the problem is my hair, not only the dark curls that fall across my face but also the fuzz on my arms and legs. In eighth grade, the other students leave in my locker a note signed by everyone in the class.

"Monster," it says. "You're disgusting." It's a notice of expulsion.

∾

The loneliness of the dead. How they are isolated by what they know about themselves and about us.

This is what I see when I look at Kantor in his self-portrait. Although the eyes appear almost shut in the drawing, the face is pointed with intensity. The artist seems to have visualized himself dying in a moment of concentration, thought. Sitting in my parents' living room after a cocktail party, I consider the knowledge held in that still face. The closer I lean into the drawing, the more I see it's not merely a composition of black ink on off-white paper. There are smudges of brown on his forehead and shoulders, the corpse already touched by dirt. And, around the jaw, some dark lines have been erased with white paint, so that the body is both a place of presence and disappearance.

Mrs. P, my history teacher, has decided that the eighth-grade class field trip to Kraków will not include the customary excursion to Auschwitz this year, although it's only an hour's drive away from the city. "She's an antisemite," my favorite teacher, Mrs. H, tells me as we eat lunch together in her classroom.

As far as I know, Mrs. H and I are the only Jews in school. I often sit with her during recess and free periods, reading while she grades papers. Or else we talk about books. Mrs. H is everyone's favorite teacher. Given how bullied I am, how much my classmates enjoy whispering "You're hideous" and "You stink," Mrs. H's popularity is miraculous to me; that she can make her strangeness so appealing to others is like the wonder of a tiny cup of oil lasting eight days when there is only enough to burn for one night. Small and rounded, with wine-red lips and a thick bob of dark hair, she is always draped in a woven shawl, gesturing at the blackboard, her movements theatrical, her voice carrying to the back row of desks. In my memory, she never speaks sternly. She laughs. Although a woman in her mid-forties, she announces "I'm twenty-nine, darling," no matter how many times the boys ask, "But how old are you really?" Mrs. H seems to me a figure of joyful comedy and good humor. One time, she gives me a taste of dried yak curd; it's a present to her from another student. And when I bite into the small, yellowed lump of cheese, it turns to sour chalk in my throat. Hacking and spitting the mouthful into a trashcan, I turn to Mrs. H.

"How delicious," I say, laughing and laughing.

On the field trip to Kraków, I cry when Mrs. P makes me share a room with my greatest tormenter, a huge Australian girl—easily a foot taller than I am—who loves to bump against me in the hallways and who mocks my name.

"John—isn't that a boy's name? Aren't you really a boy?"

Years later, I live for two months in the small town of Oświęcim, or Auschwitz, as it's called in German. On weekends, I take a rattling bus to Kraków, where, I'm amazed to learn, Mrs. H now lives. Although she is going to be away for most of my visit, she gives me a key so that I can stay in her apartment, only a short walk from the beautiful square at the center of the city.

Afternoons, I sit outside at a café. The woven backs of the chairs—"harp-shaped"—are just as Robert Pinsky describes them in "The Unseen." But unlike the characters in Pinsky's Holocaust poem, I am not making up my mind "to tour the death camp." I have already been touring them, almost compulsively; these Saturdays and Sundays in Kraków are my break from walking the grounds of Auschwitz I and II, where I watch the tourists touch the concrete dividers of the barbed wire fences, no longer electrified, this place of preserved horror with its rooms full of shoes and shorn hair, what Pinsky calls "the whole unswallowable / Menu of immensities."

In Kraków, I eat a piece of the apple cake known as szarlotka, licking caramelized juices and powdered sugar from my fingers. Every hour on the hour, there's a sound from the church spire nearby. A trumpeter plays a five-note melody, the hejnał. Always the music ends halfway through, the tune suddenly stopping. The famous explanation for this ritual is a Mongol invasion in the thirteenth century. Spotting the intruders at the gate, a sentry tried to trumpet a warning to the city. But before he could finish the song, an arrow punctured his throat.

❧

Shortly after Kantor's death, Cricot 2 performed *The Dead Class* in the United States. In a review of the production, Mel Gussow writes that "the dead return to life in order to evoke a tragic vision of the past . . . These are autobiographical and historical memories about the lifeline that brought him through the 20th century." In a place like Poland, it is impossible to say that the personal and the historical do not sit beside one another, sharing the same hard seat on a small wooden bench. A classmate pulls my hair on the playground, the bully's fingers catching in my curls, and I know that we are part of some larger theater, both of us stock characters in a play about old hatreds.

And later, Gussow writes, "a cadre of ghosts returns to a classroom. The specters take their place amid mannequins representing themselves in childhood . . . Puppets are lifelike while actors can seem like sculptural objects." This is sometimes the challenge of making art. Objects can become more solid than people, weightier in the hand, easier to render. I remember the letter that my classmates wrote to me more clearly than I recall the students who held the pen or folded the piece of paper, sliding the note through the slats of my locker. What was his name? Jeff Monroe? Geoff? And hers? Kara Johnson? Cara? And the Finnish girl with the nose that sloped upward like the sharp veering off a cliff? Marie? Mari Something. My classmates are a mist that settles on the Vistula in early winter.

∽

Is this why I love Kantor's death mask—that this object has more power than does even the memory of a cruel eighth grader from thirty years ago? Kantor continues forever on the paper. And, when my mother sends me a digital photograph of the self-portrait, I open the file on my computer screen. There's still something new to study here. Today, it is the slope of his eyelashes. Despite the rushed lines of the self-portrait, each hair seems precise and careful. Did Kantor's hand, perhaps, slow down when it came time to choose whether his eyes would remain open or whether they would be permitted to close?

∽

I am thirteen or fourteen when I learn that the American vice president is scheduled to tour Poland. The advance team has arrived and plans are already underway: what stone landmarks the visitors will see, where they will place ceremonial wreaths, with whom they will dine and in which gilded palaces. At home one night, my parents worry about the latest idea. The United States is planning to return several pieces of Judaica, artifacts of the Shoah. Wouldn't it be wonderful, the vice president's office suggests, if the objects were given back to the Polish government on the grounds of Auschwitz itself? I imagine canapés, sparkling beverages served from gleaming platters. I imagine the displays of eyeglasses piled high, the thousands of toothbrushes, the mounds of shoes, the suitcases. I picture revelry among "the whole unswallowable / Menu of immensities."

My father, in his work as the Public Affairs Officer at the American Embassy, goes often to Auschwitz. Congressmen and senators frequently include the death camp on their itineraries. But he never takes me there. I do not think it is because, like Mrs. P, he wishes to rub away the traces of atrocity. I suspect that he cannot imagine what he might say or do, if we were to stand together beneath the iron archway, "Arbeit macht frei" curving above our heads. Instead, we go only so far as Kraków, where we visit Wierzynek, a restaurant that has been open since the Middle Ages. Even in the early 1980s—what my family calls "the bad old days"—when there is nothing on the shelves and every waiter in every café and bar answers "Nie ma" (we're out), Wierzynek remains a place of plenty. In a room where the walls are covered in dense tapestries and the chandeliers glitter so brightly we can almost hear the whisper of crystal, my father and I eat a classic Polish meal. A deep red, peppered broth of beets with tiny dumplings shaped like human ears. Herring with pickled onions and sour cream. Larger dumplings formed to look like crescent moons that are filled with wild mushrooms and sauerkraut. And, finally, a layered cake of puff pastry and custard, its surface dusted with a faint snow of powdered sugar.

❧

Nearly a decade later, in graduate school, I learn to think as a scholar might about the traumatized landscape of Eastern Europe. The class, called "The Ethics of Representation and the Literature of the Holocaust," is taught by a young professor whose surname means "stag" in Polish. We study Art Spiegelman's graphic novel *Maus*, hybrid texts like W. G. Sebald's *Austerlitz*, David Grossman's *See Under: Love*, D. M. Thomas's *The White Hotel*, Binjamin Wilkomirski's fraudulent memoir *Fragments*, and poems by Paul Celan and Dan Pagis. We discuss the theorists who have helped to define this field. James Young. Berel Lang. Shoshana Felman and Dori Laub.

Several of the students speak Yiddish or Hebrew. There are many French speakers, some German and Russian, too. I am the only one who knows Polish. Of all the American Jews in the room, I am the only one who grew up overseas. When we watch Claude Lanzmann's nine-hour documentary *Shoah*, I recognize the Polish farmer who speaks about the murder of Jews off-handedly, as if he's discussing the slaughter of a cow or pig. To the other students, he's a caricature of antisemitism. But, to me, he resembles all the old men from whom I used to buy paper bags full of cherries at the local market in Warsaw. When I thanked them, "Dziękuję bardzo," they would have smiled and called me "kochana," or dear.

℥

Pani Basia—who looks after me whenever my parents miss the curfew and are forced to stay overnight at the US Embassy—is a tiny woman, barely five feet tall, her arms strong from decades of cleaning the houses of American diplomats. I learn most of my Polish from her, following her around the kitchen, beginning with the words for different ingredients, mleko, cukier, mąka, then moving to the verbs used in cooking and baking, the adjectives to describe the taste of things, their texture and scent. She shows me how to spoon batter into a pan to make the translucent crepes called naleśniki, how to lift them gently from the heat onto a blue plate. We fill them with chocolate ganache and candied orange peel or the more traditional mixture of ricotta and raisins. For dinner, she serves me my favorite, that most treyf of dishes, kotlet schabowy, a breaded pork cutlet. She always offers it to me in the diminutive form—kotletcik—which I understand, intuitively, is a way of expressing what we have come to feel for one another, just as when she tucks me in at night, she wishes me colorful dreams, kolorowych snów, before kissing my forehead and tugging the blanket up to my chin.

One time, while Pani Basia is flipping through cookbooks with my mother, she stops on a page that shows a recipe for gefilte fish. She explains that in Polish, this dish is known as karp po żydowsku, carp in the Jewish style. She can make all these things, she says, because her own mother, a farmer, hid Jews during the war. And Pani Basia's father, she goes on, was a

Jew himself—picked up by the Nazis in a roundup, what was called an akcja.

Later, when I ask my mother what happened to Pani Basia's father—if he returned after the war—my mother shakes her head. She isn't sure.

"That was the only time Pani Basia talked about her parents."

ᘓ

Scholar Magda Romanska characterizes the work of Kantor as "post-traumatic," which she argues "denotes a rupture between drama and theatre (text and performance)." I recall the Poland of my childhood, and I can't say that I feel toward it a violent rupture, although I recognize its betrayals. In February 2018, when the current Polish president signs into a law a new bill "making it illegal to accuse 'the Polish nation' of complicity in the Holocaust and other Nazi atrocities," I think of Kantor training his actors to shout, "Aleph aleph aleph." What do we know about King Solomon? Poland keeps reading from the same script, although there was once a Wielopole where the church stood across the square from the synagogue. Polish pickles have the same sourness as kosher dills. And a carp that swims in the bathtub will soon be ground up with eggs and onion, transformed into gray patties that taste of herbs and salt. Polish Jews will eat this dish on Passover, Polish Catholics on Christmas Eve.

ᘓ

In Andrzej Wajda's filmed version of *The Dead Class*, the camera does something that the eye cannot, often darting in to frame the angles of Kantor's face, his profile—the distinctive ridge of his nose—already so familiar to me from staring at his self-portrait. The drawing offers me a perspective of Kantor that I would not get if I were in the audience watching a live performance of the play. The drawing, too, is a close-up, a camera of pen and ink. The movie takes in Kantor's gestures, the way he conducts the bodies and voices of his actors, their lips pursed or puckered like comic fish.

What is a séance but a gathering in which we attempt to communicate with the departed? In *The Dead Class*, Kantor is the intermediary, introducing the audience to a cast of ghosts, spirits trapped in the limbo of Polish history. In the self-portrait that hangs on my parents' wall, Kantor is both medium and specter, the lines he sketched on paper like the planchette moving across a Ouija board. "Thus," critic Michał Kobiałka posits, "a painting could be a metamorphosis, a collage, a décollage, l'art informel, a figurative art, an object, or an abstraction." I stare at the profile Kantor has rendered on paper and appreciate how an artist can make use of the imagination: to anticipate grief, to transform the terrifying into the familiar and containable. Loss can fit inside a black frame. It can fit on a stage. The sharp teeth can be pulled from the mouth of history, each tooth held between finger and thumb like a small, white piece of chalk.

From the Archives:
Lessons in American English

Take 1

Stand still. The mic is sensitive—it hears your hands touching your hair or making gestures in the air. Your job is to make the voice a body full of movement. The voice can jump. It can skip across the grass. The voice can be a girl much larger than you are.

Take 2

For many weeks, when I'm fourteen, I stand in the padded box of a recording studio in Warsaw. Behind the glass, a Polish man is turning dials. He's signaling my silence in the room.

Take 3

I read my lines.

"Hello," I say.

"I love vanilla ice-cream, too."

"I like brown dogs."

"Don't you?"

I leave space between my sentences for someone to answer back.

Take 4

I often find myself in strange roles: soloing on the soundtrack of a Polish movie, singing the role of Mrs. Hem in Benjamin Britten's *Noye's Fludde*, sitting for an interview on Polish TV to explain what it's like to be the child of US diplomats. I don't remember how I am asked to do any of this work. I don't remember how I come to play Little Girl One on a series of English language tapes. It must be the precision of my speech. My consonants are sharpened pencil points. My vowels, round, American.

Take 5

To be more specific, my English is of no place anywhere. This is a consequence of living everywhere. I am three the first time we move to the United States. The next time, I'm eight. The next time, eighteen.

Take 6

In third grade, I am learning how to be American again. We have just returned from a posting in communist Poland. This is a world before internet and satellite TV. For the past three years, I have watched fifteen minutes of television a week, *Pszczółka Maja* (Maja the Bee), an animated show that celebrates the united workers of the hive. Maja has a head of pollen-yellow hair, her body striped in black. I know every word of the theme song in the opening credits, Maja washing her face in a dewdrop, Maja flying deep into a flower, Maja rowing a small peapod across the surface of a lilypond, Maja weeping in the moonlight. I know nothing in America as well as I've known the Maja the Bee.

My new math teacher phones my parents to complain: "You didn't tell us your child was retarded."

On the other end of the line, my parents are silent. Finally, my father answers abruptly, "What are you talking about." He is not asking a question.

"She can't solve a simple word problem," the teacher says. "If Jack has three pennies in his pocket, five nickels, two dimes, and a quarter, how much money does he have?"

"Our daughter has never seen American money before," my father says. "She's never seen American money."

On the playground, my classmates tell me, "You don't sound American." I say that I do. "You were born in Italy—you can't be American." I say that I am. "You just moved here," they say. "You're not really American." I am. I am.

Take 7

Now read the line again. Read it as if you're sledding on a winter hill. No, read as if it's warm outside, and you're traveling to the sea. Or read as if the night is full of glimmering.

Take 8

Decades later, at a concert at the Polish Embassy in Washington, DC, my parents are talking with another man and woman, all of them sipping champagne and biting into tiny crepes dotted with gray-black lumps of caviar. When the Poles hear my parents' surname, they ask, "By any chance, are you related to Jehanne Dubrow?" When my parents say, yes, that I am in fact their daughter, the couple laughs. "Our children learned English by listening to her voice."

Take 9

I am always alone before the microphone.

Take 10

I try to imagine a whole generation of Polish boys and girls echoing my words. They press PLAY to hear me sing or talk. They press REWIND to hear me say *three, that, there,* the pairing of "t" and "h" so difficult for the Polish tongue. When they're tired of practicing the sounds, they quiet me by pressing STOP.

Take 11

Let's go to the top of the page. Please, read the nursery rhyme like you're telling a funny story. Or read it like a secret. Or read it like you're remembering a small animal, which is to say with tenderness. Which to say as if you feel its fur against your fingertips, as if you hold its tiny weight.

Take 12

I have never heard these cassettes. But perhaps, somewhere in the world, my words are still encoded on slender strips of tape, stacked somewhere in an archive of displaced voices. I am speaking from the magnetic spooling of the past.

Essay, Made of Antique Glass

Brussels was the city of our comfort and languor. By the time I turned sixteen, our family had lived in many places. Belgrade. Zagreb. Lubumbashi. Washington, DC. Warsaw. The District of Columbia again. Warsaw again. And now Brussels, with its wide avenues and gilded cafés. Our house, on a little corner of street in a green neighborhood, had an elevator and a tennis court, both of which made us feel as if we were visitors to some grander life. Driving ten minutes from home, we might have arrived in the municipality of Waterloo, passing the tall grassy mound—a pointed hill, really—crowned with a bronze statue of a lion. This was the site of that famous battle between Napoleon and Wellington. We seldom stopped, driving on instead to a cheese or bread shop. Ten minutes in another direction from our house was a restaurant that specialized in *moules-frites*, the national dish of Belgium, mussels served in great cast iron pots and the fries accompanied by a small dish of mayonnaise.

After our years in Warsaw, Brussels felt like falling onto a smothering, luxurious featherbed, my parents back from the US Embassy by dinnertime, no strikes or Martial Law or history rioting on our doorstep. Brussels was the city of divided languages, of red tape and paperwork. The closest we came to difficulty was one August when my father walked to Mary Chocolatier, an official supplier of chocolate to the Belgian royal court, only to discover the store closed for the summer holiday, the ballotins of dark pralines gleaming behind locked doors. The closest we came to deprivation was when it rained too many days in a row, the sky that same low gray one might find in a painting by Brueghel.

I am thinking lamplight

through the branches, blossoms
dark against an amber sky.

I am asking what curve
of tango-orange? What's held
in the cupping hands of glass?

✑

On the rue Américaine, my mother and I visited the Horta Museum, designed by the Belgian architect Victor Horta, and built between 1898 and 1901. We often went on these kinds of excursions in Brussels; I was a junior in high school by then, past the worst years of adolescence and relieved to live in a place where I wasn't teased and bullied for my strangeness. For me, Brussels was coffee and a slice of cake filled with passion fruit mousse. It was an afternoon at the movies and a bag of candied orange peel robed in dark chocolate. It was my first sip of raspberry beer.

I was so grateful for the pleasures of Brussels, how seldom anyone looked at me on the street. In Poland, my black hair and dark eyes had marked me as foreign—was I Roma? was I a Jew? In Brussels, I could be the one doing the looking. In the cool cream light of a gallery, I could stand in front of a surreal nude, her body turning from skin to summer sky. Or I could regard the Brueghel painting that Auden once described, with its tall, spindly ship sailing past a pair of white legs protruding from the indifferent sea. Or, inside the Horta Museum, I could look and look— how everything was coiled, flowing shapes of tile, wood, and metal that evoked the bent gestures of flowers. A skylight arched above me. The brass railing of a staircase curled against my hand.

The aesthetic movement known as Art Nouveau began in the 1880s and lasted until the start of the first World War. Art historian Cybele Gontar explains that Art Nouveau "endeavored to achieve the synthesis of art and craft . . . encompassing a variety of media." Depending on country and language, the movement was called Art Nouveau, Jugendstil, Secesja, Modernismo. Art Nouveau was interdisciplinary, its bent lines interpreted on paper, cast in precious metals, cut in stone, printed on fabric, and blown in glass, its influence visible in music, dance, and literature. By the beginning of World War I, it had been supplanted by Art Deco, whose forms were more streamlined to evoke the sleek, modern world.

When we lived in Poland, every piece of art that my mother and father purchased came directly from the artist, and with it came a small story: the artist smoking in a studio filled with leaning stacks of paper, the contacts made through a friend of a friend, the payments of dollars sometimes accompanied by a bottle of vodka. But, in Belgium, my parents bought mostly from antique dealers, their gaze turning toward the French vases and bowls once produced by Charles and Ernest Schneider, whose glass creations married Art Nouveau to Art Deco.

Founded in 1913 but only resuming regular production in 1917, near the end of World War I, Schneider Frères & Wolff is known for its two product lines: the abstract, swirled compositions signed "Schneider" or "Schneider France" and the acid-etched glass forms signed "Le Verre Français" or "Charder." Sometimes the bases of Le Verre Français pieces were also embedded, patriotically in a nod toward the tricolor flag, with a tiny strip of red, white, and blue glass known as a candy cane.

In Brussels, my parents bought out of intellect rather than emotion, although this is not to say that the objects acquired weren't exquisite. Schneider glass is full of hazy light and lightness, sometimes streaked to look like marble or jasper. In her survey of Schneider glass, Edith Mannoni writes that these pieces were not only large but heavy, and "making them required physical strength as well as skill." Le Verre Français is defined by its elaborate designs—symmetrical orchids, berries, beetles—etched into layers of fused glass, creating the effect of a cameo, a pairing of the translucent and the opaque.

It was always an event when my parents returned with a new piece. Sometimes the object came to visit for a short while, placed prominently on the dining room table so that my parents could study it from different angles at different times of the day, deciding if they liked it enough. I wanted everything to stay. The tall vase, its base shot through with purple the color of an old bruise, a pink-yellow sunset at its rim. A wide-mouthed bowl perched on a fine stem, nearly black at the bottom and a blazing tangerine up top. Greens. Blues. All the synonyms of red and orange. The weight and airiness, a visual paradox. Glass, nearly an inch thick, and the kind of heavy that required two hands to lift.

To collect glass—this was not a practical pursuit for our family. Each time we arrived in another country, we discovered that something had broken in transit, no matter how carefully wrapped and cushioned. Perhaps my parents' sudden interest in Schneider and Le Verre Français was one of the first indications that they were tired of all the packing and unpacking, the new streets to navigate, the new languages to learn; after Belgium, we would have only one more posting abroad, in Vienna, where the people seemed even unhappier than in Brussels. A family that owned so much valuable glass could not keep traveling, not if we wished to avoid minor damage or outright shatterings.

ᴇⁿ⌾

I am thinking of a flask
in a laboratory of the beautiful
turned azure radiant.
I say more flowers on a slender
neck, more midnight
fronds across a golden day.

ᴇⁿ⌾

Charles Baudelaire hated Brussels. In an outline of a book he had planned to write about Belgium, the poet says of the city: "Cigars, vegetables, flowers, fruits, cuisine, eyes, hair, everything *bland*, everything sad, flavorless, asleep. The human face itself, blurred, clouded, asleep." He writes, "Belgium is a monster. Who would want to adopt it? And yet it contains within itself *several* elements that could contribute to its dissolution. This diplomatic harlequin could be torn apart from one moment to the next." This was the 1860s. Belgium had been a country for a little over thirty years, "patched together," as scholar and translator Richard Sieburth puts it, "by the Great Powers in 1830 and therefore Europe's newest, and most rapidly modernizing, artificial nation state."

Three decades later, in *Heart of Darkness*, Joseph Conrad calls Brussels the "whited sepulchre," a Biblical reference to Matthew 23–27: "Woe unto you, scribes and Pharisees, hypocrites! for ye are like unto whited sepulchres, which indeed appear beautiful outward, but are within full of dead men's bones, and of all uncleanness." Later in the novel, Conrad's protagonist, Marlow, returns to Brussels and is disgusted by what he sees. "I found myself back in the sepulchral city resenting the sight of people hurrying through the streets to filch a little money from each other, to devour their infamous cookery, to gulp their unwholesome beer, to dream their insignificant and silly dreams."

In these same years of Baudelaire and Conrad, King Leopold II was transforming Belgium into a country of enormous wealth, thanks to his ruthless extraction of resources—rubber, copper, ivory, diamonds—from the Congo Free State. Art historian Debora Silverman writes that "[b]y 1905, two decades of contact with the Congo Free State had remade Belgium as a global hub, vitalized by a tentacular economy, technological prowess, and architectural grandiosity."

The buildings that my mother and I toured in Brussels, with their gold-leaf façades and murals of languorous women leaning in a haze of decorative smoke, were constructed in an era of what Silverman describes as "unprecedented economic prosperity." With the support of "elite patrons and some budgets awash in Congo dividends," architects like Victor Horta could design the edifices of their fin de siècle dreams.

I regarded those Art Nouveau structures with an uncritical tenderness, admiring the agile curves that defined the aesthetic, coup de fouet—the whiplash style—so alive with motion and energy. Those afternoons when my mother and I walked through the polished rooms, my eyes consumed each ornamented surface. It was the same kind of joy with which I considered puff pastries and tiered slices of cake at a local café.

Silverman explains that "the whiplash style provides visual equivalents of two foundational elements of the regime in the Congo Free State: the rugged, relentless, and sinuous coils of the Congo's wild rubber vines, hailed as 'vegetable boas' with 'veins of gold,' and the imperial chicotte, the long flogging whip at the center of Leopold's rule." In all those years, I never saw what I was seeing. When we visited the Royal Museum for Central Africa, established in 1898, I studied the plundered masks and stolen grave markers, the winged insects pinned to walls, the combs carved from wood, the photographs and illustrations. In 2018, after an extensive renovation that attempted to decolonize such exhibits, the Museum reopened. But when I was there during the early 1990s, the Museum was still a place that celebrated Belgian imperialism. In those rooms, standing among all the spoils of Leopold's brutal reign in the Congo—a rule defined by slaveholding, mutilations and beatings, rape, murder—I never thought about the nearby Art Nouveau buildings, that they were artifacts of the same vicious era.

"And this also has been one of the dark places of the earth," says Marlow near the start of *Heart of Darkness*. He is speaking about the Thames. He goes on to imagine "very old times," when the Romans first arrived in England, a landscape of "[s]andbanks, marshes, forests, savages . . . utter savagery." The point is not that places like London or Brussels were once wilderness and then became cities of grand squares and towering archways. The point is that their gleaming palaces were beautiful containers for violence.

∽

                    I say breath suspended
          in glass is heavier than
                    breath contained by body—
                              those glistening bubbles
     locked within a world
               of hardened crystal light.

∽

My father tells me that, in early 1994, my mother would often come home from the Embassy and recount her worries over dinner. "Something terrible is about to happen in Rwanda," I can almost imagine her saying. And when I returned to Brussels from college in late May, the one hundred days of slaughter were well under way. My mother—daughter of Jewish refugees, whose family fled to Honduras in the late 1930s because they couldn't get visas to enter the United States—had stopped using a word as imprecise as *something* by then. She said "genocide."

Imperial Germany was the first European nation-state to colonize Rwanda. But at the end of World War I, Belgium took control of the region. The Belgians, preserving the structure created by the Germans, allowed the Tutsi minority to remain as the ruling class over the Hutu majority. In her landmark study *Leave None to Tell the Story: Genocide in Rwanda*, historian Alison Des Forges writes that "[b]y assuring a Tutsi monopoly of power, the Belgians set the stage for future conflict in Rwanda." By 1961, when Rwanda achieved independence, the country was highly divided along racial lines. Just as they had under Belgian rule, all adult citizens held identity cards indicating whether they were Hutu, Tutsi, Twa, or naturalized. In 1994, these bureaucratic documents would prove helpful when it came time to start killing people. Identity cards were used at roadblocks and other points of access to determine who would be permitted to pass and who would face the machete or the masu, the club studded with nails.

At the dinner table, my mother often talked about the diplomatic cables coming in from Washington or from Kigali. Searching the internet nearly three decades later, I come across a declassified cable with the heading "RWANDA MONITORING GROUP." It's a summary of just over a week's worth of State Department cables, starting April 7, 1994, and running through April 15. The day before these cables begin, an airplane carrying the presidents of Rwanda and Burundi was shot down over Kigali. In timelines, this event is frequently identified as a critical point that marked the start of the genocide. As journalist Mark Landler succinctly points out in an article from the *New York Times*, the downed plane allowed the United States to "take the lead" in advocating for the withdrawal of UN troops from the region. After this, "the crisis rapidly escalated into one of history's most grimly efficient genocides, with some 800,000 people killed in less than 100 days."

My mother's name is listed five times in the declassified document. Here is her first appearance, in a dispatch full of typos and misspellings:

```
04/08/94  03:30   Call from Brussels to RWG Leonard
                  Jeanette Dubrow of Embassy Brussels
                  reports that the BE gove
                  rnment will decide on evacuation
                  plans @ 5 am.m Washington t
                  ime. Dubrow reports some talk of de
                  nationalizing Belgian tr
                  oops serving in UNIMIR if the UN
                  won't change their mandate.
                       The Embassay asked the BFM to
                  satay in clos touch with the
                       U.S. and the French. 10 BE UN
                  AMIR confirmed killed.
```

And here is her last, even briefer, seven days later:

```
04/15/94  07:23   Jeanette Dubrow from Embassy Brus
                  sels phoned Task Force.
                  Informed Coordinator that there is a
                  report on Flemish
                  T.V. that UNAMIR forces at Kagali
                  airport are coming under
                  fire from both forces of both sides.
```

The document stops with this entry:

```
04/15/94  19:00   Coordinator phone Embassy Bujumbura
                  to inform them
                  that the Rwanda Task Force was offi
                  cial disbanding.
```

I read the declassified text and try to imagine myself in my mother's position, making dispassionate phone calls or typing out reports in the cool, spare language of bureaucracy, even as she saw that, at the highest levels of the US government, the choice was being made not to intervene. She has said, "sometimes it's important to try doing good from within the system." Once, during the worst of the fighting, she stayed on an open phone line for nearly ten hours with journalists who were trapped in a hotel in Rwanda, until a contingent of Belgian soldiers came to rescue them. Sometimes the connection crackled over the long distance; at other moments, she told me, the call was "crystal clear," the sound of shooting in the background.

At home, my mother used the word genocide, just as she had the year before, when the White House spoke about what was happening in Bosnia as ethnic cleansing. "During the early weeks of slaughter," explains Des Forges, "international leaders did not use the word 'genocide,' as if avoiding the term could eliminate the obligation to confront the crime." I remember my mother telling me that, on Rwandan radio stations, the Tutsi were being called cockroaches, inyenzi, insects that must be driven from every corner and hole, must be stamped underfoot. "Like the Nazis," she said, "who called Jews vermin."

Ten years after the publication of *Leave None to Tell the Story*, Des Forges wrote of Rwanda that "not since the Holocaust had we seen civilians massacred so rapidly, so systematically, and with such a blatantly genocidal objective. And yet national governments and international institutions refused to intervene, backing away from a crisis that was politically complex but morally simple."

Long before I read Auden's "Musée des Beaux Arts," I often visited Breughel's *Landscape with the Fall of Icarus*, perhaps one of the most famous paintings displayed in Brussels's Royal Museums of Fine Art. Like the speaker in the poem, I too was attracted to the tension between the ordinary elements of the artwork and the extraordinary. "In Breughel's Icarus, for instance: how everything turns away," Auden observes, "[q]uite leisurely from the disaster." The line break after "turns away" briefly emphasizes the menace of this scene, before the sentence continues onto the next line and we are returned to the farmer doing his work in the fields and the sun shining everywhere. The poem, after all, was published in 1939, another moment in which many were turning away. The pain of Icarus means nothing to the wealthy vessel floating by. Falling and drowning, the boy barely makes a sound. And the ship keeps moving, no doubt on its way to a port, where it will let off passengers who have pressing business, affairs of commerce or state.

ↄ

To scratch the surface

                                        of shimmering. To shape
                            the breakable into a switch.
There's a place where acid cuts

                            away the surfaces and leaves
                                        the shape of wings.

ↄ

"The dead at Nyarubuye were, I'm afraid, beautiful," writes Philip Gourevitch in his book about Rwanda, *We Wish to Inform You That Tomorrow We Will Be Killed with Our Families*. "There was no getting around it. The skeleton is a beautiful thing. The randomness of the fallen forms, the strange tranquility of their rude exposure, the skull here, the arm bent in some uninterpretable gesture there—these things were beautiful, and their beauty only added to the affront of the place." Here is one of the problems with the beautiful. It exists, even adjacent to horror. And the writer, confronting this fact, finds his language conceding as well, words made lyrical despite themselves.

I study a Schneider vase displayed on a shelf in my parents' home. I look for signs of atrocity there, the glass neck tapering to a narrow opening, its molten orange like lava poured into a mold. I think Debora Silverman is right when she argues that the provenance of the whiplash style of Art Nouveau can be traced to the "wild rubber vines" of the Congo and to the chicotte as it lashes against skin. But, still, the vase remains beautiful. "I'm afraid," Gourevitch says, because he understands that his admission is indecent. The eye should not see loveliness in a site of genocide.

Having walked through the rooms of the Nyarubuye Roman Catholic Church, where approximately twenty thousand people were once massacred, Gourevitch leaves the building with his guide:

> [M]ore bodies were scattered in the grass, and there were stray skulls in the grass, which was thick and wonderfully green. Standing outside, I heard a crunch. The old, Canadian colonel stumbled in front of me, and I saw, though he did not notice, that his foot had rolled on a skull and broken it. For the first time at Nyarubuye my feelings focused, and what I felt was a small but keen anger at this man. Then I heard another crunch, and felt a vibration underfoot. I had stepped on one, too.

The crunch and vibration. The fury that Gourevitch feels, first toward his companion and then toward himself. Gourevitch is telling the reader, look, I will show you genocide, but I will have to tread on bodies to do it. The writer may construct beautiful sentences, but he also becomes responsible when he stands so close to the bones.

Suffering, as Auden tells us, occurs close by. It happens while we are living our human lives, eating mussels or climbing the spiraled staircase of a historic house. The corner of the living room where my parents now display their collection of Schneider and Le Verre Français is bright with carefully positioned spotlights. The illumination makes it easier to study the details of each piece. I can examine how blue slides into green and then to a chartreuse the exact shade of certain cats' eyes. I can look closely at my favorite, a vase shaped like an Erlenmeyer flask, conical and thin-necked. It is adorned with cobalt flowers that have been acid-etched on turquoise. The light is strong enough that, when I slide my finger along a sloped edge, I can almost see there what Leopold did in the Congo Free State. I can lean in and blow on the surface of the glass. I can try to breathe away the gray silence of dust.

Snapshots / Warsaw, 1987

[When Oma flies across the ocean to visit us, she smells of face powder, violets and roses crushed to dust. Her purse smells of rumpled tissues. It smells of peppermint candies filled with chocolate cream. It smells of dollar bills and Deutsch Marks and złoty, all that paper and the touch of strangers' hands.]

[The Vistula smells of mermaids lifting ancient swords above their heads. Old Town smells like new construction, cut wood and layers of paint. Łazienki Park smells green in summer, silent and white in winter like the blank page of a book.]

[Pani Basia's armpits smell of sweat and powdered sugar. When she tucks me in, I rest my face against the flowered pattern of her dress.]

[Theodora Bear smells of my mouth pressed around her nubby ear. She smells of plastic button eyes. Favorite Blankie smells mostly of sleep but also of night terrors, the sudden cry that tears out of me in the early morning dark.]

[My parents smell of paperwork. Of stuck at the Embassy, of emergencies and cables sent from America. Sometimes, on special evenings, my mother smells of smoke and carnations from the lacquered bottle on her vanity. I like to stand in the drowsy cloud she leaves behind.]

GALLERY THREE

Mother and Child

They're carved from a single block of linden wood, the sculpture so tall and thin that I've often worried it might fall from its table, her dress a sky of glinting stars, and the child seated in her arms, touches of gold reflecting around the outlines of each face to remind us she's a mother, yes, but something more as well, the boy already heavy in her arms, crowned with the weight of prophecy, and the wood so wanting to be touched that most days I still place my finger on the bow of her tender mouth, remembering the Polish carver who gave me this piece thirty years ago, after he saw in my father's office a small watercolor I painted when I was eight—yellow roses leaning in a porcelain vase—and how he told my father that I *was an artist already*, already an artist, I would remind myself when curled in the introspection of my bed or standing at the window to watch a winter tree gone leafy-thick with birds, the sculpture a figure that in secret I began to pray before, not bending to a god, but to the hand that held the carving knife, the hand that removed nicks of wood to reveal those holy bodies underneath, and to the hand that dipped a brush in blue and red, and even to the hand I heard had lost a finger, the blade slipping like a warning to watch out, that beauty is a sharpened thing, and how decades later, for a time, I turned the sculpture to the wall, so that the mother's tinted eyes wouldn't watch me from across the room, having told my own mother I didn't want a child, because how could I choose a baby's craving mouth when I would rather search for synonyms for hunger—need, for instance, or longing almost liquid on the tongue—and my mother crying then, although I asked her how, if language were a slab of wood waiting for a knife, how could I not slide my palm along the knotted surface, not search the grain for what was held inside, how could I do anything but cut.

Portrait on Metal with Patterned Scarf and Streak of Light

The photographer's studio is on wheels, hitched to a pick-up truck, and parked today beside a Dallas tattoo parlor. At one end of the room, she has placed a wooden stool and three lights on adjustable stands. At the other end is a door to a tiny darkroom where she prepares the chemicals. I watch as she sets up for our appointment. "I don't use cyanide," she tells me. "And I don't use cadmium." But other than that, the techniques are essentially the same as the ones used in the mid-1850s. "Tintypes," she says, "were the first time that the working class could afford to get their picture taken."

She cleans the surface of a piece of metal that has been coated black. Next, she pours a slow stream of liquid onto the dark rectangle. "Collodion," she explains, a gelatinous substance that contains salts which will absorb the silver; it's still used "in the medical field" and was once employed as a "wound dressing." She tilts the metal, so that the excess collodion drips back into the bottle. I hear the clinking of containers being opened and shut. I see a jar labeled POISON, a skull and crossbones hand-drawn in black marker on the glass. "This stuff, if it gets on your eye," says the photographer, nodding toward one bottle, "will make you go blind."

While the metal plate is left to dry to a tacky finish, she turns on the lights, each one on its own stand. And, now "the composition of the photo." I sit on the stool, while she shifts the beam toward and away from me, until she finds the right level of glare. One of the lights shines inches from my right cheekbone.

This isn't the first time I have been placed at the center of a triangulation of brightness. Four or five years ago, I posed in front of a range of neutral backdrops, tilting my head, lifting or dropping the corners of my mouth, widening my eyes. There was a make-up artist who applied many layers of foundation and powder, a soft glow of highlights, a lipstick the exact shade of my lips. After I picked my favorite from the proofs, the photographer edited the final image on his computer to fade the vertical indentations around my mouth, what are known as marionette lines. He whitened my teeth by a shade. He sharpened my jaw. To achieve an author's headshot that seems both natural and perfect requires time and artifice.

In the tintype studio, everything feels a little less staged. There are no backdrops. No one is penciling in the shape of my mouth. Instead, I keep noticing the collision of old and new, how the camera is a wood box from "the late 1800s" mounted on a tripod from "the 1970s or '80s." Once the composition has been finalized, I am told to sit very still while the photographer loads the plate in the dark room. When she returns, I see the plate has been placed inside a kind of frame that will soon be slotted into the back of the camera.

We decide I will smile in the photograph. She will count to three, my lips and teeth moving into position by the time she arrives at the last number. She lifts a piece of fabric at the back of the camera, bends her head beneath it (*like in the movies*, I think).

"Your head is in the perfect position."

"Hold still," she says.

The sound of creaking and loading.

One. Two. Three. And then a tremendous POP. A sharp flare.

Later, I'm amazed to see that my face stayed motionless, my eyes relaxed. I am sure I must have flinched at the surprise of the flash bulb's great noise.

And now we are both moving. I slide off the stool. She brings out a small rectangular tub filled with water and begins to pour a jug of liquid over the metal plate, which sits in the basin. I hold my phone from above, so that I can film the change from darkness to image.

My face melts into being. The next day, when I watch the video I have shot, I see the process takes less than 30 seconds, the plate at first a haze of silver-blue with patches of shadow, then everything dividing into areas of black and white. Liquid swishes over the abrupt appearance of my skin.

And there I am.

The photographer points to the distinct scrolled pattern on the scarf around my neck, the perfectly glimmering coils of my curls. "The detail is limitless. You can zoom in infinitely because there's no grain," she says. "All that's left is where the light touched the plate."

In the tintype, despite the halo of imperfections at the edge of the metal and the streak of brightness in the top left corner, I don't look as if I've been carved from another century. It's the same face I've seen in selfies, in formal studio photographs, in snapshots. I had hoped to find a version of myself transported from an earlier era. In the tintype, I can see a few wrinkles on my forehead, the imperfect roundness of my cheeks. There's nothing of the 1800s etched into my features. This disappoints me. But why? Why would I want to locate myself in the past? I had expected a transformation that didn't occur. But why did I hope for it?

In *Camera Lucida*, Roland Barthes argues:

> The portrait-photograph is a closed field of forces. Four image-repertoires intersect here, oppose and distort each other. In front of the lens, I am at the same time: the one I think I am, the one I want others to think I am, the one the photographer thinks I am, and the one he makes use of to his exhibit his art.

Examining the tintype, I feel the bruised intersection of these four "image-repertoires," as Barthes call them. What pierces me is that I cannot believe this face is who I am or who others think I am or who the photographer does or what kind of ordinary art I've been made into. My nose is a crooked stub. My eyes have none of the ambered quality that will hold the glance of another. I am plain, not only to myself but also, apparently, to the photographer and to any viewer who might consider this image.

I am often disappointed by the person I see in pictures. Last year, a kind and gifted photographer took new headshots of me. I stood in a local bar, leaning against a wall of exposed brick, while he clicked and clicked. *Yes*, he would say. *Beautiful*, he said, laughing from behind the camera so that I couldn't help laughing along with the flirtation of his lens. When he sent me the proofs, there were dozens of my smiles. But I could only see the roundness of my jaw, the places where the day was unkind to my skin.

The more I study the tintype, the more I realize it's my smile that has failed me. When we view black and white photographs of our great grandparents in the old country, when we look at strangers posed in high lace collars, we know they come from the past by the severity of their faces. They seldom smile, no doubt because of the long exposure required to capture these images. A closed mouth is easier to hold before the slow, searching stare of the camera.

A tintype demands stillness. A person who sits for a tintype portrait must be almost frozen in the moment of the plate's exposure to light.

How different this is from contemporary thinking about photography; now it is the camera that must keep up with us, must catch the blurring gestures of arms and legs. For our wedding, my husband and I hired a photojournalist who shot celebratory events in her spare time; I liked the semblance of spontaneity in her work. In one of my favorite pictures, I am mid-laugh, my head tilting back, my arms wrapped around Jeremy, the two of us crushed in the middle of several concentric circles of wedding guests dancing the hora. This photograph is evidence that smiles are a thing of quickness and change. They are enlivened by their transience.

I always smile in photographs. I learned early on that others thought mine lovely. *What a beautiful girl*, guests would tell my parents, as I looked away, pretending I hadn't heard. My father taught me how to smile on cue for the camera, how it's possible to lift one's features into the swift proof of happiness. As the daughter of American diplomats, it was useful—I discovered—to be able to smile on command at official events, a photographer snapping casual shots for the public record or telling clusters of people to turn toward the lens. When I look at pictures from my parents' years in the Foreign Service, I notice my father's teeth, the confidence and decisiveness of them, that large smile overwhelming all the grim adjacent faces. If I were to open my wallet right now and remove my driver's license from the narrow pocket, I could point to a similar expression. Those teeth. The disarming force of that grin. Yes, I can summon a smile, even in bleak bureaucratic spaces.

As Roland Barthes explains, our awareness that we are being photographed transforms us "in advance into an image." Sensing the camera's presence, we alter ourselves. "I feel that the Photograph creates my body or mortifies it, according to its caprice," writes Barthes. In my case, that creation or mortification is the smile. Even away from the camera, I have transformed myself in advance of the image, my smile a form of concealment at dinner tables, in conference rooms, and on the street, a way of making others think my mind is less of a cutting thing. In particular, I use the smile on men, knowing its dazzle. It conceals a sharp edge. And I have seen what happens when I drop the smile, the way one might drop a glass on the floor. The falling. The shattering. The smile is a fragile vessel, but it holds reassurance. *I am not a threat*, it seems to say.

Of course, there is the occasional picture in which I am solemn. Many years ago, I had my portrait taken for a newspaper interview titled "For a Navy Wife, First Panic, Then Poetry." I am staring large-eyed into the camera, the burgundy collar of a coat pulled high around my neck. My mouth is a thin line. How dour I look. How unrecognizable to myself.

For nearly four decades, my father has carried a photograph in his wallet. The paper is curled at the edges, worn from the friction of rubbing against dollar bills and other currencies. In the picture, I am five. My shirt is pink, the couch cushions damask. I hold a black-covered booklet. My body is the posture of a reader, so intent on the words in front of me that I don't seem to realize I'm being photographed, that my father is standing only a few feet away, that this image of me will last beyond the impermanence of the sofa, the bobby pin in my curls, the paisley drapes hanging in the top right-hand corner of the snapshot. The photograph is composed in the way of a painting from the 1800s; it recalls Mary Cassatt's diaphanous pastels of women and girls bent toward the pages of a book, the world a swirl of close reading. Here, I do recognize myself. This is one of my daily expressions, not so much gloominess but concentration, the creased brow that signals thought. In some ways, it is my ideal image: unaware of external lookings, too absorbed in the interior life of language to feel the burden of another's scrutiny.

But this is the exception. Most of the time, I am smiling. Every morning, to document the clothes I wear for my social media account, I stand in the brightest corner of the dining room, my left hand tucked in a jacket pocket, my right hand hanging at my side, and hidden in my palm a remote control approximately the size and width of a pinkie finger. On the table in front of me stands a tripod, perhaps twelve inches tall. It holds my cell phone in the spring tension of its grip. When it's time to take the picture, I press the round button of the remote control with the edge of my thumb, a touch so tiny that the camera does not observe my movement. I click and click. I shift the angle of my chin. I open my mouth to the right size of smile—after months of practice, I have learned that this amount of toothiness, this degree of tension in the muscles of the face preserves whatever beauty might still be mine.

When I have enough shots, I swipe through them on my phone. The mistakes—the droop of an eye mid-blink, my chin pressed into Shar-pei wrinkles—disappear in the time it takes me to touch the miniature icon of a trashcan. Delete. Delete. Delete. Like this, with only the tap of a finger to glass, I disappear myself.

"People want the idealized image: a photograph of themselves looking their best," writes Susan Sontag in *On Photography*. "They feel rebuked when the camera doesn't return an image of themselves as more attractive than they really are." We fear, she says, "the camera's disapproval." According to Sontag, the first technique for photographic retouching was introduced in the mid-1840s. "[T]wo versions of the same portrait—one retouched, the other not—astounded crowds at the Exposition Universelle held in Paris in 1855 . . . The news that the camera could lie made getting photographed much more popular."

And, in the end, don't I want the lie? Scholars like to speak about the gaze, a regard that comes from someone else. A gaze can shape the body, what the body wears to be desired, how hair is pinned back to show the alluring taper of a neck, the naked collarbone below. The gaze decides how a body is interpreted as studious or virginal or debauched—a matter of glasses, perhaps, a string of pearls, a black seam dividing the back of a leg from hem to pump. But what kind of power do we have over ourselves? The most tyrannical form of looking might be the self-gaze, as when I say, *the roundness of my jaw, the places where the day was unkind to my skin.*

I may long for the lie. But I also distrust the accomplice of my smile. It collaborates with the camera. Its curve seems to indicate I am a baby doll with articulated limbs. I am a girl waiting to be asked to dance. Or a woman who's hoping someone will buy her a drink. Or confused and in need of an explanation. Or weak and wanting help with her luggage. Or someone whose voice goes high with uncertainty at the end of every sentence. *Smile*, a stranger has told me on the street. And whether I choose to obey may determine if he follows me for the next few blocks, calling out, *hey hey hey.*

Over the past year, my teeth have been begun to fail me, too. The first time was in my office on campus. I shut my mouth and suddenly felt a jagged piece of stone on my tongue; it was half of a lower molar, broken off after almost a decade of pounding contact with the hard porcelain crown on the tooth above it. "Like a chisel," my dentist said, "striking and striking." Next came two more crowns. An infection in the gum. "Let's wait and see," the endodontist told me, when it seemed I might need a root canal. Then I had a deep cleaning. "It's like scraping barnacles from the underside of a boat," my dentist said.

All those long afternoons leaning back in the chair, a blue paper bib pinned around my neck, I thought about Freud. According to my yellowed copy of *The Interpretation of Dreams*, it's very common to dream about teeth. "Dental stimulus," he calls it. "To represent castration symbolically, the dream-work makes use of baldness, haircutting, falling out of teeth and decapitation." Sexual repression leads to "transposition," the mind shifting its anxieties from the provocative lower half of the body to the safer, less discomfiting upper half: "[I]t becomes possible in hysteria for all kinds of sensations and intentions to be put into effect, if not where they properly belong—in relation to the genitals, at least in relations to other, unobjectionable parts of the body."

But I'm not dreaming. And what I worry most about is a mouth full of emptiness. If dreams of tooth loss represent castration and feelings of sexual powerlessness, what does the actual loss of teeth mean? I look in the mirror and worry, not only that I'm witnessing the end of beauty but also about my diminishing ability to control how people see me.

No wonder when the photographer sends me the digital scan of my tintype, I immediately want to pass the image through an array of digital filters. Can I make myself more attractive? Might there be a gauzy glow or an artful blur that could transform this picture into what I wanted?

Instead, I download an app for my phone. It allows the user to transform any photograph into a tintype, its tagline, "Selfie like it's 1899." Once a picture has been taken, the app converts it into black and white, decreasing the depth of field. As with a real tintype, the digital image appears rough and decomposing at its edges. I take a fake tintype of my dog. She is reduced to a black nose in a cloud of gray fur. I turn the camera on myself and, after many attempts, I finally achieve something like what I hoped for in the tintype studio. My eyes are ghostly and pale, the center of focus.

I remember how I used to love looking at a black-and-white photograph of my mother taken when she was nineteen. That was the year she won a beauty contest, the prize a scholarship to study in Madrid. In the picture, she is a perfect composition of pale skin, her shoulders sloping toward a sweetheart neckline, her hair not quite beehive but a series of wound coils. All the exquisite adjectives could apply to her. Alabaster. Shimmering. Luminous. She looks of the more recent past here, like a mid-century movie star.

It is possible that, with the right hairdo and the correct positioning of lights, I could achieve some of my mother's dewy smoothness. But what I desire is a less curated beauty. In a tintype, a face is permitted its wrinkles. And because we are seeing hard-lived history, the people who sat for these older portraits are viewed as entitled to their pockmarks and creases. They've earned the right to asymmetry. They are beautiful, despite the absence of make-up, filters that turn their features radiant, despite the fact that they do not know the twenty-first-century craft of tilting their heads to pleasing angles, do not ingratiate the viewer with a smile. In some real, unedited way, they are beautiful. This is what I tell myself.

Earlier I asked *Why? Why would I want to locate myself in the past?* The answer, I suppose, is to know whether I am beautiful. It's a matter of vanity. But also a way of knowing what weapons are mine.

Already, in my mid-forties, I wonder where my features are going. "All that's left," the photographer told me in her studio, "is where the light touched the plate." Is this what aging means—that the light will no longer touch me? I feel my face undeveloping. It's like watching the short video of the tintype I shot, this time played in reverse. I am submerged in a basin, my features clear beneath the glass transparency of water. And then there is shadow. A stream of liquid lifts from the pan back into the pitcher. In less than a minute, my face spreads out in ripples. The plate returns to its silvery haze, until only the still sheen of metal remains.

Snapshot / Washington, DC, 1986

[Soon the insects would come up from the ground. It said so in the news-paper. After seventeen years—five longer than I had been alive—the cica-das would tunnel upward from sleep into the hard touch of daylight. And a few weeks later, they rustled everywhere, a sound like crumpled cellophane. They sat on the wrought iron railing outside our door, on the sidewalk and the lawn, out on the street where the cars crushed them by the hundreds. They climbed the trunk of the apple blossom tree, their translucent wings fluttering the pink-white petals like a breeze in miniature, their eyes red seeds. At school, one of the boys found a pair held together in winged desire, joined end to end, and tore them apart in a gesture so quick I knew he had practice making this kind of hurt. When he threw them both at me, I tried to brush the ripped bodies from my shirt. All afternoon I could feel them crawling across my arms, and I wanted to be outside myself, to no longer be touched by the twitching legs. I could feel their longing to be linked again and the rough fingers yanking wingtip from wingtip. I ran the whole way home, the trees alive with thrumming, all the uncoupled alone among the leaves.]

Lost Vessels

Years ago, I went to an exhibit so beautiful that, for months after, I dreamed about the ancient ceramics displayed behind glass. They were all colors and sizes, decorative and practical, formed on the wheels of Japanese potters across many centuries. I remember a bowl so large it could have been used to bathe a newborn, although its walls were the thickness of a leaf in early April and the same translucent green. I remember shades of clay layered like earth on top of earth. I remember something glazed a cornflower blue, as if blossoms had been turned vitreous and permanent.

But a long time later, when I tried to find evidence of what I'd seen—an old newspaper article, a photograph, perhaps—I couldn't locate anything, not the year or the name of the show. It was as if all proof of the exhibit had disappeared. The ceramics existed now only as glistening shapes. There, in the barely lighted rooms of imagination, I could open one of the cases and remove a cup, hold its roundness in the echoing curve of my palm. I could circle my finger along its edge.

ভ৯

Beyond the ceramic objects I'd seen, I could remember the building that housed them: The Arthur M. Sackler Gallery. Along with the Freer Gallery of Art, the Sackler forms what is now known as the National Museum of Asian Art. These days, it takes a series of deliberate clicks through several hyperlinks on the Smithsonian's website to find the page where Arthur M. Sackler is described as "the principal benefactor of the museum that bears his name." He was, the biography continues, "a physician and medical publisher" who "devoted his professional career to the advancement of medicine." The site explains that Sackler's "other passion was collecting exemplary objects from Asia, which evolved into the collection that forms the foundation of the museum's holdings."

℘

People who knew him well described my cousin as *sweet*. They said of Adam *sweet boy*. Even once he was an adult, his features still retained a slight roundness. And maybe it is kinder to think of him as always young, sucking his thumb, falling asleep against his older brother. Remembered like this, he remains a child, his hands unable to twist open a plastic bottle with its safety cap. He is forever years away from his first opioid.

℘

No one would have called Arthur M. Sackler sweet. His presence—on museum signs and in promotional materials—is less visible than it once was, as if a heavy curtain has been drawn across the man. In 2019, US Senator Jeffrey A. Merkley wrote to the Smithsonian Institution, asking that the Sackler name be removed from the gallery and arguing that the family "hooked thousands of Americans on OxyContin through aggressive and misleading marketing tactics and profited from one of the deadliest public health crises in our country." In that same year, the Louvre erased references to the family from an area known previously as the Sackler Wing of Oriental Antiquities. The National Portrait Gallery chose to turn down a £1 million gift. The Solomon R. Guggenheim Museum, the Tate, and the Metropolitan Museum of Art decided they would no longer accept donations from the Sacklers. And the National Museum of Asian Art—while legally prohibited from striking Arthur M. Sackler altogether from its edifices—undertook what news articles described as a "large-scale rebranding effort."

Here's the thing: it's best not to remind museumgoers, as they stand before a lighted display of pale jade cups and bowls, that the Sackler name has come to mean OxyContin. It's hard to take pleasure in beauty when one is distracted by thoughts of powdery white extended-release tablets, pills that the FDA warns can put a user "at risk for overdose and death." Even taken at the correctly prescribed dosage, a patient is "at risk for opioid addiction, abuse, and misuse that can lead to death." Unused OxyContin, the FDA advises, should be flushed down the toilet, as a safety precaution.

ᕦᕤ

When I think of OxyContin, I'm inevitably led to thoughts of my cousin. My mind, hazy and uncertain as smoke, drifts to him.

I barely knew Adam. If I try, I can more easily summon an image of one of the lost vessels from that vanished exhibit at the Sackler Gallery than I can my cousin's face. When he does appear clearly, it is his large hands I remember. They hold a peanut butter sandwich or finger the red stitches of a baseball. People are meant to touch or be touched, unlike precious objects in a museum.

Sometimes my writing forgets that.

ᕦᕤ

Purdue Pharma released OxyContin, its version of oxycodone, in 1995, eight years after Arthur M. Sackler's death. An article I read takes great pains to—notice the idiom I use so carelessly here, *takes great pains*—to emphasize that "Arthur Sackler died several years before his younger brothers, Raymond and Mortimer, launched Purdue Pharma, the company behind OxyContin. He is not named in any of the current lawsuits against the company." But as journalist Patrick Radden Keefe explains, Arthur did own a third of Purdue Frederick, the company that would one day become Purdue Pharma. He built his own wealth on the marketing of pharmaceuticals. "As both a doctor and an adman," writes Keefe, Sackler understood that "selling new drugs requires a seduction of not just the patient but the doctor who writes the prescription."

His tactics could be dishonest, and he possessed a genius for identifying ways to increase demands for a drug that might otherwise have limited applications. In the 1960s, for instance, he developed a campaign that "encouraged doctors to prescribe Valium to people with no psychiatric symptoms whatsoever." Decades later, Purdue Pharma would employ a similar strategy with OxyContin, downplaying the drug's potential for addiction while persuading doctors that the medicine "should be prescribed not merely for the kind of severe short-term pain associated with surgery or cancer but also for less acute, longer-lasting pain." OxyContin, as an analgesic to be used in palliative end-of-life care, would have a limited patient base. But as something that might muffle the hurt of cracked vertebrae, swollen finger joints, and generalized muscle aches, well, this was a drug that could generate billions of dollars.

☙

Most of what I remember of Adam comes from childhood, when my family used to visit my grandmother at her condominium in Miami. I can picture him in those rooms of dense brown carpeting and gold-mirrored walls. He had rounded cheeks and coiled blonde curls. As a very little boy he liked to suck his thumb while leaning against his big brother, with his free hand twisting a strand of Jeffrey's hair around his finger. Adam was gentler in those moments, his sturdiness softened. Although three years younger, he easily outweighed me and was several inches taller. He could be rough. An only child at the time, I wasn't yet used to the bruising play of boys and often ran from his contests. When we played thumb wars— *one, two, three, four, I declare a thumb war*—he pinned down mine much longer than the obligatory three seconds, my fingers turning pale beneath the pressure of his grip. I ran from Jeffrey as well, who preferred taunts over physical demonstrations of power. He could make me cry with a few whispered words. "What a baby," he said. Or sometimes, "Stupid girl."

Their father was still around in those early years, laughing somewhere in the background of every room. David was always talking about *the game* and using expressions I didn't understand: the odds, action, over-under, the spread. He was the kind of man who looked most at ease in the clamor of a party, a glass of some liquid seated in his palm, the ice cube sliding from side to side with any wide gesture of his hand.

Once, I asked my mother what she thought of my uncle. We were sitting close together on a white plastic chaise beside a swimming pool, while she rubbed white smears of sunscreen into my arms. I watched the swish of water, wishing I could leap into the turquoise glittering where my cousins already splashed, making brief tidal waves with the thrash of their bodies.

"That man could charm a snake," my mother said. She drew a line of sunscreen down the length of my nose. If she had anything to do with it, I would never burn, never enter the pool without the floating safety of water wings. "He could charm a snake," she repeated.

While his big brother Jeffrey had their father's quick way with words, Adam had David's coloring, a golden tan, the same bold nose. Soon their father would be gone, their parents now divorced. Aunt Susan—or Aunt Susu, as I call her—would be left to raise two sons on her own.

❧

Writing this essay, I experience the difficulty of re-creating Adam—the way he held a melting ice cream cone, the shelves of sports memorabilia in his bedroom, how he laughed. The words are pieced together slowly. Memory is not kintsugi, the Japanese art of repairing damaged ceramics with a mixture of lacquer and powdered gold. There are ugly seams. There is no glittering dust poured into the fractures between sentences.

❧

At seventeen, Adam went to a school in the wilderness for difficult adolescents. As we moved into adulthood, I heard occasional stories about him, my mother offering brief updates over the telephone. He was lifting weights and sober. No, he was back in rehab. No, he was working out and healthier every day. My memory of these stories is as faint as smoke lingering in an empty room. I don't know what led him to the pills. A sports injury? A car accident? My mother recalls one part of the narrative (his time in prison), and I another (when he got out on bail). Once, too, I asked my father what he remembered about those times. We were eating lunch, and he jabbed his fork at a translucent slice of onion. "I don't know," he said. His numbed response was an answer, I suppose, something to do with the guilt one sibling might feel toward another, my father's life so fortunate when his sister's was so full of grief. The sharp tines scraping against the plate, the onion glistening with pearlescent tears—these weren't images of silence but of what my father seemed unable to say.

If I'm honest about things unsaid, I'll admit that I can't bring myself to call Aunt Susu. I could ask her about the specifics of Adam's twenty years of addiction. But I prefer incomplete memory. I wonder if she does, too.

∽

In "Bride in Beige," Mark Doty explains why an essayist might choose to leave a recollection inchoate, the page not always a site of certainty but of mist and blur. Questions, he writes, were central to his memoir *Firebird*, including questions that his own sister could have answered. "*Why not just ask her?*" noted an editor in the margin of the manuscript. "I hadn't *wanted* to know," Doty realizes, choosing instead to be "allegiant to memory"— even its inconsistencies and failings—"not to history." He observes that "some memoirs are more interested in the process and character of remembering than others; in these, it sometimes feels that memory itself is a *form:* associative, elusive, metaphoric, metonymic."

∽

Now a grownup, Adam shaved his head to pale brown stubble. He wore tiny diamond studs in his ears. For two decades, Adam was both broad-shouldered and breakable, a man who in my imagination was solid as cast bronze but also a piece of porcelain, fragile and porous. It was easy for me to turn away from him the way I might move quickly past an unsettling piece of art in a museum. And I didn't want to study my own hurts or to be studied myself, that I too might be an object perched on an acrylic pedestal in a sealed case.

Not long before he died, shortly after another stay in rehab, Adam told his mother, "I don't think I can get out from under this. No matter how much I take, it's never enough."

He was dead at thirty-seven.

❧

In a press release about the sentencing of the doctor who prescribed Adam oxycodone five days before his death, the US Attorney's Office of the Middle District of North Carolina explains that investigators learned the physician "was prescribing opioids to known 'drug seekers' with little or no examination and for cash." And although he is never named in the press release, I believe the next sentence refers to Adam: "One person . . . died in 2016 from Acute Combined Drug Toxicity." I suspect this is Adam because an article in the *Charlotte Observer* states that he "died from 'Acute Combined Drug Toxicity' on Aug. 28, 2016," and that "An autopsy conducted by the Miami-Dade County Medical Examiner revealed a combination of oxycodone and alprazolam were [*sic*] the cause."

According to the newspaper article, Adam went with Jeffrey to see the doctor, explaining "that he did not have back pain; rather he was addicted to pain pills." I can imagine the brothers sitting together in the scuffed waiting room of the Care Plus Urgent Care. Maybe on the wall there was a poster of a blue sky and written across the clouds in dark letters, *We Care About Our Patients!* Maybe there was a dim aquarium in the corner, a single fish flicking its tail through the water like a strip of tattered rubber. I can imagine other patients in nearby plastic chairs, some sitting very still, others tapping their fingers on their cell phones. That place, I think, would have been very cold, the air conditioning always set high enough to the rustle the fronds of the potted palm. The room would smell of fear-sweat, sharp and sulfurous.

❧

My mother's fibromyalgia. The arthritis in my father's fingers. My old injury from the years I rowed crew in college. The slipped disk in my husband's spine. Each of these sufferings could have led to OxyContin. If any of us had ended up seated across from Adam's doctor, we too might have left the office ten minutes later with a prescription folded damply in our hands.

☙

At first, the doctor prescribed my cousin Suboxone, a medicine used to treat adults addicted to opioids. Suboxone is meant to be "part of a complete treatment program that also includes counseling and behavioral therapy," says Indivior, the company that produces the drug. I wonder about Adam's treatment program. Did he have health insurance? Was he able to sit with a therapist every week, the two of them talking in the pastel light of an office? Did he hold a crumpled tissue? Did he stare down at his sneakered feet? I wonder if one day he said, *fuck this*—and who could blame him—OxyContin notoriously difficult to quit, wrenching the body with withdrawal, the coughing and sweat and hand tremors, the crawling of ants across the skin—blameless, unblameable, if he decided instead to sit on his patio drinking a beer and watching a gecko skitter across the tiles, its spotted body elusive and quick as thought.

Apparently, for "reasons unknown, in January" the doctor began prescribing oxycodone again. This, too, seems like a *fuck this* moment, the physician pulling his prescription pad from a drawer in his desk. For "reasons unknown," the article says, but how, I want to know: what made Adam's doctor scribble Oxy once more? Was it indifference or callousness or greed? Again and again and again, the doctor tore a prescription from the pad. More and more *fuck this* moments. I can hear the quick sound of tearing and the soft shhh of the paper placed in my cousin's hand.

The doctor is in prison now, sentenced to forty-six months and fined $50,000. He pleaded guilty to six counts "of knowingly causing to be distributed oxycodone, a schedule II controlled substance, while acting outside the course of professional practice and without a legitimate medical purpose."

In "The Promotion and Marketing of OxyContin: Commercial Triumph, Public Health Tragedy," Dr. Art Van Zee writes that Purdue Pharma "promoted among primary care physicians a more liberal use of opioids," which in turn led to the "increased availability of all opioids as well as their abuse." Purdue Pharma pathologized pain, persuading both doctors and patients that all pain could and should be avoided, completely avoided; with the right dosage, it could be medicated into nonexistence.

Imagine that: a life emptied—like a bottle—of its pain.

❧

This is what I do in trying to compose a more complete image of Adam. I read a report from the North Carolina Medical Board that revokes the doctor's license and states that he acknowledges his own "failure to conform to the standards of acceptable and prevailing medical practice." I cross-reference court documents, including a memorandum in which the judge denies the former doctor's recent motions for compassionate release. I wander through these many documents online, each one like a bright, cold room in an exhibit on addiction. My research leaves me with a clearer understanding of my cousin's dependence on opioids in his final year but not a real picture of who he was.

❧

On some days, when it feels like a stone has been placed behind my shoulder blade, deep in the muscle, I lie on top of a hard rubber ball, pressing against it until the twinge begins to dissolve. I take ibuprofen, although I know the danger to my liver. When the stone is unbearably sharp beneath my skin, I drink a glass of wine.

At such times, I understand why someone would want to erase pain, even if that first erasure might lead to the disappearance of other sensations, too. Eventually, the whole person might disappear.

Is this what Adam wanted? He must have hurt so much.

When I was fourteen, I stayed with Aunt Susu for a few days. In the afternoons, Jeffrey's buddies would come over to play poker. I watched the teenage boys seated in a circle on the floor. Their legs had outgrown the rest of their parts; cross-legged, they resembled piles of pick-up sticks, their limbs haphazardly thrown. But when they placed their bets, tossing plastic chips into the center with a flick of the wrist, they were suddenly graceful, less gangly than before.

During one game, Jeffrey lost very badly to a friend. "Don't worry," the other kid smiled in a way that was meant to indicate his munificence. "You can pay me next time." Jeffrey nodded. I bit my lip to keep the surprised *oh!* inside my mouth. They were playing with real money, not pink and blue rectangles of board game currency. I squinted at the scrap of paper on which my cousin wrote in ballpoint pen, *IOU $110*, signing his name at the bottom. For him, this kind of loss was normal, I realized. The debt was nearly as much as I earned in three months of allowance.

Adam watched beside me. He was, Jeffrey declared, too young to join the game. Adam commented on every card. "Yes!" he exclaimed, or else, "Dammit!" He leaned toward the circle of taller boys, wanting so much to be a part of their strange agreement to owe and be owed, to bet and to risk. His face was still rounded like a child's, cheeks flushed as though he had just come indoors after pitching baseballs at the fence. Adam held a spare pack of cards, which he had removed from the shrink wrap. A shriveled glob of clear plastic lay on the carpet a few inches from the trashcan; this, in my memory, is an image I can hold onto, almost photographic in its clarity. Sometimes he squeezed the whole deck in his fist. Sometimes he rubbed a finger across the sharp sides of the varnished paper, a gesture that reminded me of how I loved to stroke the deckled edge of a favorite book.

Watching the boys play poker made me feel as if I'd been running around the track during gym class, dizzy, trying to catch my breath. But it seemed to evoke in Adam a different emotion. On his face, I saw what looked like happiness. Want.

❦

I had searched for corroboration of the exhibit of Japanese ceramics I attended so long ago. I found no proof of it in newspapers or magazines. Did the lack matter? I don't need documentation to know I held my breath in the Sackler Gallery. I moved softly between the displays, afraid the weight of my footsteps might tremble a vase. I can still see that blue glaze gleaming on the bright surface of the porcelain.

And were my recollections made more vivid by reading articles and press releases that named (or didn't name) Adam? Not really. The documents provided me with dates, the name of a doctor, the results of my cousin's autopsy. I learned about Acute Combined Drug Toxicity. I learned about the fatal interactions of opioids and benzodiazepines.

I could ask Aunt Susu for more.

But this isn't a historical record. Memory is a form, as Mark Doty says. Mine is chipped at the edge. It has a hairline crack running through it.

დ

Beyond the fact that we were cousins, what was my relation to Adam? Why can I more easily evoke the inanimate ancient artifact than I can the human being? Truth is, I know very little about Adam because I wanted the glass between us. For so much of my life, he was an artifact—first of boyhood, later of addiction—that I chose to consider from a comfortable distance. To come closer would have required me to examine how I was connected to the terrifying, muscular child and how I was also linked to the man who took up so much space with his wide, bruising shoulders. When we were little, his strength frightened me, his fingers smothering mine as we played together. *One, two, three, four, I declare a thumb war.* When we were grown, I was afraid to feel anything about him at all: fear or, worse even, love.

დ

And, finally, although I'm uncertain of what she'll say, I do ask my Aunt Susu about Adam. "I remember so little," I tell her on the telephone. "I want to write what I don't remember."

"I shut down things too," she says. But then she is talking and talking, how in the courtroom the doctor "didn't look at us, didn't turn," how when his sentence was handed down, his wife "was just crying and crying" in her seat up front. And more memories, then: the addiction and when it started, the arrest in his twenties, the pills, two hundred pills a month, each month a visit to the doctor and a five-minute meeting to pick up the next prescription. I'm typing. I'm attempting to keep up with the swirl of her speech, her voice moving so quickly through the haze of years. Already she is telling about when he came home that last time from rehab. It was a Thursday, and she found him dead in his bedroom Sunday morning. "At 10 a.m., he was out of it," she says. She looked in on him, his body tangled in the covers. "Of course, I feel guilty—I saw his chest moving, and I shut the door." Barely an hour later, she went back in. "And that's when I could see he was blue." Terror. So many phone calls—*He's dead he's dead he's dead.* Jeffrey will not speak about his brother, she says, will barely stay in the house where Adam died. "I never stop talking about him," she tells me. And his father, David, now wears his son's name inked in Hebrew letters on his forearm, the opium-dark script of lamentation.

֍

Tonight, I've returned to the website of the National Museum of Asian Art. I consider the history of heroin, the fields of poppies, their seedpods scored and oozing sap, the smoky dens, the wars between nations. In the long rectangle of the search engine, I type the word "opium." There are five results. One is labeled "opium pipe bowl." I click on the link. From the Qing dynasty, 19th to early 20th century. It's ceramic, characterized as "Stonewear with white glaze," although it looks more cream than white, its surface mottled with black specks and reddish streaks.

The bowl is listed as "currently not on view." The irony of this object is a thick, choking fog. Maybe there have been others who, thinking of the Sackler family business, searched the Museum's website for references to opium. Someone, I suspect, must have decided this thing should not be displayed. Or it could be that the collection of the Arthur M. Sackler

Gallery is so full of exquisite items there's no need to exhibit a little ceramic piece such as this. Among the precious porcelains and other artifacts, its value must be negligible, barely worth the room it occupies in a glass case. On the screen it appears huge. But its dimensions are listed as 3.7 by 6.7 centimeters. In other words, it's tiny.

Hard to believe something so small can cause so much death. For a moment, the thought stops my fingers' movement across the keyboard of my computer.

Of course, a pill is even more minute. A pill slips so easily down a throat. A pill, ground to dust, is light as breath. Dissolved in water and injected, a pill slides swiftly to the vein.

This bowl, at least, is attractive. I do admit its appeal. It was carefully designed to fit on a metal ring which was then attached to a pipe made of bamboo or lacquered wood. It is simple and ingenious. It has a small hole at the top to hold a bead of opium paste. A strip of cloth would have been used to form a tight seal between the bowl and the pipe, some rough scrap of fabric that ensured no vapor could escape.

I imagine someone must have handled this once, fumbled to fix it securely. The touch, I suspect, was not always delicate. Perhaps the bowl was dropped or cleaned too roughly. It might have been misplaced in a shadowy chamber. That a ceramic vessel should come through so much heat undamaged. That it should survive the agonies and collisions of the world. That it should outlive a body. I don't know how it has managed not to break.

Snapshot / Lubumbashi, 1978

[I am guessing from the thinness of my mother's face that I must have been almost three when the picture was taken. I have to guess, because I lie outside the frame. Perhaps I was asleep, curled tight against my blankie, its silken edge kissed softly to my hands. Or else I stood at the French doors that looked out onto the backyard, a place I was not permitted to wander—there were mambas coiled in the grasses, vipers the color of spring leaves. She would have been thin from breastfeeding me well past the usual age that, in those days, pediatricians permitted. I had almost died of some tropical disease; I fell ill during the rainy season when the tin roof of our house was the sound of thousands of fists knocking. A small baby, the sickness made me smaller. "Keep her on the breast," the doctor said, "and bananas, as many as she will eat." For decades after, I couldn't smell the yellow fruit without choking on what I remembered of its taste, banana mashed with the back of a spoon, banana crushed to softness on a plate. I can't recall the breastmilk, although the doctor said it saved my life. The photograph shows only my mother's face, which even here is beautiful, the amber light a tenderness against her skin. My mother is smiling. She is smiling as if the body is not a pane of glass, as if the body is a sheet of metal and nothing can get in.]

On the Color Matching System; Or, Marriage

467 U	½ pt Rubine Red
	¼ pt Process Blue
	1⅛ pts Yellow
	28⅛ pts Transparent White

Six years into our marriage, I decided to paint the bedroom a pale brown. He was often away—deployed, out at sea—and when we spoke on the telephone, we said "fine" and "fine." Sometimes I forgot the shape of his nose. When he came home, I couldn't remember how to close even the smallest distances: for instance, how to walk across the kitchen or place a cup of coffee in his hand.

What I wanted instead was a wall of sand or to fall asleep in a grain bin, something to drown in.

380 U	3¾ pts Yellow
	¼ pt Process Blue
	12 pts Transparent White

We bought our first piece of art on our honeymoon. In the printmaker's house, we stood together, hip to hip, sliding open deep metal drawers to study the pieces stored inside.

It was hard to pick a favorite. We chose a landscape marked with the silhouettes of winter trees, bare branches placed against a hillside of many purples, and the horizon turning yellow-green.

When he bent close to examine the details of the print, I touched the skin at the base of his neck. I told myself, *this too belongs to me.*

Of course, there was little about him that I possessed, just as I couldn't claim, every spring, the forsythia bursting suddenly into flower beyond our window.

226 U   10 pts Rhodamine Red
                         6 pts Rubine Red

Today, when I fan open the formula guide in my hands, it occurs to me that, although love itself has no formula, I could match each moment of my marriage to a certain color. I might say last August was a faded blue, like a pair of blue jeans worn to softness. Or I might find a carmine and call it the weeks we stayed in Santa Fe, how the mountains blushed at sunset. There was a year made entirely of gray. I try not to speak of it, although sometimes it shadows me when I walk our neighborhood. On our wedding day, we stood beneath a chuppah sewn from tiny scraps, our faces tinged burgundy and pink, our joy the mingling of Rhodamine and Rubine Red.

317 U   ½ pt Process Blue
                         ½ pt Green
                         31 pts Transparent White

A month ago, we hung a new painting near our bed: a house set against a pale background that swirled uncertainly with mist.

Process Black U

How can I describe the seventh year? It was more than made entirely of gray. That year was a cloud opaque with weather. It was asphalt darkening with rain. It was ink unmixed with any other shade.

Once, during the worst of it, we argued in the night. I was sobbing, "Why?" Or maybe he asked "Why?" because marriage can be this as well, two people positioned in the same room, each of them talking to a wall gone almost black as a smudge of graphite pencil.

1555 U	2¼ pts Yellow
	1¾ pts Warm Red
	28 pts Transparent White

But there were also the peaches we bought at a roadside stand when we were twenty and twenty-one, so many years before the proposal and the wedding and all the arguments that came later, some of them almost insurmountable. Maybe he asked, "Are you hungry?" Maybe I shouted, "Look!" pointing at the wooden crates of fruit.

We shared then the intimate sweetness of a peach, his bite covering my own.

2736 U	8 pts Violet
	8 pts Reflex Blue

Many afternoons for many years, I stood in the letterpress studio and spread ink across a plate of glass. It took time to mix two tints into something new, pressing the flexible edge of my knife—one side of the blade, then the other—until the pigments began to combine. First there were streaks. Rubber-based inks resist giving themselves to another, as if to blend is to lose the self. After a few minutes, I could see the inks changing like a sky gone to early evening, not a loss at all but something new, the blue merging into violet and violet into blue.

Seventy-Seven Steps

1. It was designed to withstand knocks and blows, the biting waters of the sea—

2. the 1006 Navy Chair, first built by Emeco, the Electric Machine and Equipment Company, in collaboration with Alcoa, the Aluminum Company of America.

3. Commissioned in 1944 by the US Navy to be used on military vessels, the chair is light enough to lift with the tip of one finger.

4. It is made entirely of salvaged aluminum, its surface faintly reflective. Despite its appealing design, even what I would call beauty, the chair's first obligation is to endure.

5. The silhouette of the 1006 Navy is reduced to the essence of chair: a straight back supported by three vertical slats meeting at a crossbar, a square seat gently contoured, four narrow legs joined by spindles, nothing extraneous or decorative.

6. Estimated to last 150 years, this chair will outlive me. And so much else as well: songs, cities, most books.

7. When I used to visit my husband onboard a destroyer or cruiser, I saw the Emeco chair in offices, staterooms, and mess decks, seemingly ageless and impervious to rough handling. I liked its chilly gleaming. The brushed finish looked almost soft, and yet I knew the recycled metal to be nearly indestructible. One day, I told myself, I would position six of these same chairs in our dining room, the metal an appealing contrast to the pale wood of our table.

8. In those early days of marriage, I often pulled my military dependent ID card from my wallet to study there my husband's rank and

pay grade, his DoD ID number. In the top left corner was a tiny facsimile of the Great Seal of the United States and, alongside the eagle's claw full of arrows, an almost illegible photograph of my face.

9. Dependent, from the Latin "to hang from, hang down," as if I were one of those tags that swung from a metal chain around my husband's neck. I had no rank or pay grade of my own. On my ID card, only the blurred image of my face belonged to me. The rest was my husband's information.

10. Who was this man in service khakis I loved?

11. And who was I who loved him?

12. If the chair were wood rather than metal, such a piece might be found in an old farmhouse in Virginia, almost early American in its profile, cut from simple tools, its sheen the result of many hands having touched it over decades, pulling it back from the table, wiping crumbs from it, rubbing its edges in a moment of thought.

13. In fact, Emeco now sells a wood version of the 1006 Navy. In a choice of walnut or oak, it is nearly five pounds heavier than the aluminum model.

14. Eames Demetrios, the grandson of renowned designers Charles and Ray Eames, once shot a short film about the 1006 Navy Chair.

15. In the film, *77 Steps*, there are close-ups of sheets of metal cut into ever-smaller strips.

16. Metal bent at keen angles. Metal welded to metal. Metal ground and clanking, clicking against itself, submerged in a salt bath, heated, metal brushed to the sheen of a foggy mirror. Metal anodized to an almost-diamond hardness.

17. At the end of the three-minute movie, each chair—having been constructed in a process with 77 distinct steps—is wrapped up and sealed in a sturdy box, shipped off, no doubt to a big city restaurant or hotel, this object having become in the past twenty years a symbol not of war but of upscale design.

18. Let me name another chair formed during war: the Eames LCW, which stands for Lounge Chair Wood.

19. The first time I sit in the LCW, I am surprised how well I fit.

20. The molded plywood flexes slightly. Rubber shocks are mounted where they can't be seen to bear my bulk.

21. As soon as I forget I'm sitting in a thing that seems too light and low, too artful to hold a body up, I feel the comfort of its contours against my spine.

22. The LCW looks more like a sculpture than a place to place oneself. The grand sloping of the seat and seatback are joined by the curve of a brace beneath, with all three pieces perched on legs.

23. Although the LCW was first released in 1945, at the start of a new peacetime, Charles and Ray Eames began experimenting several years earlier with the technology that would be applied eventually to the production of their iconic chair. As part of the war effort, they constructed an inexpensive splint of bent plywood to be used by American medics on the battlefield.

24. While metal splints vibrate, often causing more damage to the wounded, plywood moves with the movements of those hurt bodies that are carted away from the fighting.

25. The splint resembles a giant tongue depressor, the plywood gone golden with age, small holes poked in the rounded shape where the device would have been fixed to a leg.

26. The original splints can now be purchased from antique dealers for approximately $1,600.

27. The LCW, although sheathed in a veneer of glistening walnut or ash, is still identifiable as plywood, too.

28. Demetrios writes that, after WWII, "Charles and Ray continued to refine an idea that became a pillar of their design process: the 'honest,' or unselfconscious, use of materials. In other words, if a chair was made of molded plywood, it should show the molded plywood, not try to conceal it, and honor the plywood's inherent qualities."

29. Kneeling to study the edge of the LCW, I count the individual layers—the plies, pliable from the French *plier*, to bend—that have been glued and then pressed together, heat reforming them into the contours of a chair.

30. And when I place myself in it, I feel the slight give of the materials. Sitting in the LCW, my muscles untense. I am shielded by its

structure. The chair is true to its origins, a thing designed to protect an injured soldier dragged from the field, dragged across ditches, dragged through dirt, while horror ricocheted nearby or exploded with shrapnel.

31. Wood as softness. Wood as safeguard. Wood carrying the weight.

32. But the 1006 Navy doesn't offer shelter.

33. Its metal frame never warms against skin. The seat back permits only a rigid, vertical posture. It demands military precision from the one who sits on it.

34. This is a chair intended for long hours of work, a sailor situated before an instrument panel in the machinery room, watching gauges move or not, watching the warning lights flash or not.

35. And here is another chair made during war, this one created by the Danish designer Jens Risom. It's low to the ground and is meant for lounging. Its frame is unstained maple, a crisscrossing of thick cotton tape woven in and out to form the seat and back.

36. Jens Risom's lounge chair was the result of wartime rationing and scarcity. It's constructed with as little wood as possible, and the cotton webbing originally came from surplus parachute straps.

37. The chair was so important to Risom's career that it figured prominently in his *New York Times* obituary: "Defined by sharp Scandinavian lines and fused with the rustic aura of Shakerism and American arts and crafts, the armless, affordable chair that became Mr. Risom's signature in 1942 was one of the first mass-produced modernist furniture pieces introduced in the United States and not Europe."

38. The chair, characterized in the designer's obituary as "perhaps too humble to ever be described as a masterpiece," doesn't take up much space. It is mostly air and the absence of materials.

39. When I sit in the Risom chair, I can imagine that I have been falling and falling, its seat the only thing that slows my descent.

40. It would be easy to sleep in its organic shape; the wood has the same curve as a figure in recline, and the webbing is neither too taut nor too slack against the body, stretching just enough to reassure.

41. Our dog, Argos, loved the Risom chair more than any other object in the house.

42. By the time Argos was full-grown, he had discovered that the seat was the perfect height on which to lay his chin. He often stood beside the chair, flattening his face against the webbing, his brown, expressive eyes following us as we tried to avoid his gaze. The gesture meant *time for a walk* or else *come play with me.*

43. Risoming, we called it.

44. Argos's silence was maddening, that he could lean against the chair for ten or twenty minutes, still as a piece of furniture himself. In this patience, he most resembled his literary namesake, the dog who waits two decades for Odysseus to come home: ten years while the king helps win the Trojan War, followed by another ten as he follows a twisting, god-plagued path back to the island of Ithaca. Argos lives just long enough to see Odysseus limp through the palace gates, wearing the disguise of a beggar.

45. We knew our dog's name would be Argos, long before my husband brought the puppy home.

46. We met as undergraduates in our senior year, at a college that calls itself the Great Books School. There, *The Odyssey* is the second text all students read. The first is *The Iliad.*

47. If *The Iliad* teaches what it means to be a soldier gutted on the battlefield, then *The Odyssey* illustrates what happens when a warrior gives up on combat. *The Iliad* begins with rage, *The Odyssey* with the tears of Odysseus, the king attempting to return to a family of strangers, his wife Penelope and his now-grown son Telemachus.

48. Nearly a year into our marriage, my husband and I were finally living together in the same state, sharing for the first time a bathroom sink, a couch, a kitchen table.

49. Soon, he would be given a new billet and sent to a new ship, perhaps in Norfolk or Bahrain or Yokosuka.

50. I would be the patient wife, and Argos would be a sentry, the way dogs often are, waiting for Odysseus. In those years, I wrote so many poems about our roles, even speaking in the voice of Penelope, who weaves her vigilance into a shroud.

51. After our own Argos died, we moved the Risom chair from a prominent place in the living room to a corner of the office, where we wouldn't have to look at it every day, be reminded of the furred warmth now absent.

52. Here is what I understand: war can lead to innovation. Think: canned food and menstrual pads. Think: the ballpoint pen. Think: all the novels and poems I have spent decades reading.

53. I understand this, too. Innovation can entice the eye. It can be well and wisely formed, crafted from materials we might describe as being *honest* or having *integrity*. Innovation can produce a chair so attractive—reduced to the purest form of chair qua chair—it becomes a status symbol. *Oh, this*, a homeowner might say, gesturing as though with indifference at the costly piece of furniture in the corner, *why, that's an original Risom, circa 1943*.

54. But what to feel about these attractive chairs, emerging, as they did, out of the effort to rescue the bleeding and the bandaged, out of scarcity and collision?

55. Sometimes I am grateful for the elegance of such objects. They are lyrical in the way of a line of verse.

56. Or I feel—what should I call it?—amazement that horror can lead to ingenuity.

57. How creative, I think, that parachute straps were repurposed to make a woven seat.

58. It's easy to delight in the unforeseen discoveries of war, the fact that constraints and deprivations once led to an aluminum chair so durable it could be thrown from the fourth story of a building without suffering a dent.

59. It is more difficult to ask myself:

60. Why have I brought the traces of war inside my home so willingly?

61. For many years, my husband's uniforms hung in our closet, khakis and coveralls, summer whites, dress blues so dark they could be mistaken for a shade of black. I often pressed my finger against the lacquered opacity of a shoe to leave my print behind. I liked to take down, from the top shelf, the plastic tacklebox where he stored his ribbons and medals. I would lift the lid, admiring the

box's simple but clever design, the trays sliding wide open, tiered like a tiny staircase, to reveal their contents. There were dozens of compartments filled with objects—striped or gleaming, oak leafed or starred—whose meanings I still don't know.

62. Of course, I do know why I have been so eager to bring the war inside my home, its ghosts and whispers.

63. Because, for nearly fifteen years, I was married to the military, as the saying goes. That's what we say: *married to the military.* The expression is synecdoche, a part standing in for the whole, my husband not merely himself but a piece of the larger machinery. The chairs, too, are synecdoche, each one a little portion of war, the care that is needed to cushion bodies, the imperative to bear all burdens and blows, the vertigo of tumbling from the sky.

64. Because I have loved my husband, even when I haven't understood what service made him.

65. Made of him.

66. Makes of him.

67. Even now, two years after his retirement from service, I can still see the contours of his training in the daily rituals.

68. It is there in the way he scoops a mound of shoe polish from the tin. He rubs the darkened cloth across the leather, small circles of shadow erasing every scuff. His movements are precise and practiced. By the time he finishes, the boots have a regulation shine.

69. It is there in the creases he irons in a shirt. It is there in his early waking, minutes before the clock begins its sharp alarm. Long after her husband returned from the war, Penelope, too, must have seen Troy in the gestures of Odysseus's hands.

70. Sometimes I imagine a short film that documents all the tiny steps that made my husband.

71. There are closeups of Officer Candidate School. A body bent at keen angles. A body ground and clicking against itself, a body submerged in water, a body overheated, a body running in the fog.

72. At the end of the three-minute movie, the body is sent to stand watch aboard a minesweeper. The body is sent to an engine room on a cruiser where it kneels in the grease and oil.

73. But I wouldn't want to watch that film.

74. Instead, let me show the two of us sitting together at a table. There is breakfast. I reach across with a fork to a pierce a bite of pancake from his plate. He steals a sip of my coffee. If borders remain between us, they are more permeable since his retirement. Somewhere in another room, the news plays on the television, the sound of war faraway and small.

75. He no longer wears a pair of clanging tags around his neck, the metal stamped with his name, social security, blood type, religion. I have a passport and a driver's license. There is nothing in my wallet to identify me as dependent on this man.

76. We face each other.

77. And, perhaps, when we shift in our metal chairs, the faint smell of bitter rising from our coffee cups, we feel the surfaces beneath us, materials that have been soldered or ground. The chairs have been tempered. Remade. They don't deny where they came from or what they are, products of their histories, however hard and unyielding.

The Lodger

In the museums, tourists hold out cell phones in front of them. It's as if the twenty-first-century body requires a small intermediary between itself and any artful object. We can no longer encounter the beautiful directly but must keep it at arm's length, slowly revolving toward and away from it, our eyes directed at the pixilated screen in our hands, our thumbs on the icon of a red button that will allow us to snap the picture.

Everyone is turning and clicking. Then there's a quick glance at the phone display to make sure an acceptable reproduction of the art has been acquired before the next turn, the next click. Under such conditions, it's hard to tell how much contemplation occurs.

I remind myself that my own pointing and clicking is different. If I wish to write all this down, then I must have a record of what I have viewed. I must produce these images so that I can render them accurately with words.

I have come to New York to avoid thinking about my marriage. I will take in as much art as I possibly can over the next five days. I say *take in*, because I like to imagine that what I see will come to reside inside me. The goal is to see how much seeing I can do, how many exquisite guests will make of me their home.

If I am filled with seeing, then I won't have room to stand back and examine this fact: for a short time now, I have been out of love with my husband. Whenever I hear his voice in another room or watch him sitting across the table from me, I wonder, *where is it going—my love for this person?*

At the Cloisters, I walk through rooms transformed into the late afternoon of a distant European abbey, the light contemplative. I move through courtyard after courtyard, touching the columns adorned with flowers, creatures open-mouthed or gazing toward the heavens. In one small square, I notice a placard identifying three or four pillars that all originated in the same Benedictine monastery. What initially feels like a cohesive, creamy whole of tranquil stone is, in fact, a persuasive collage of relics from Medieval Spain or France, a composition of disparate objects.

And, yet: the luminous faces of saints; the day glittering amber and ruby through stained glass; the room of woven unicorns, their muscular bodies almost seeming to move across the tapestries; ceilings arching upward; the coolness, in the summer heat, of marble salvaged or taken from somewhere far away; a rosary bead carved out of boxwood, as the placard explains, "with astonishingly minute detail"; more saints; dozens of hands and feet bleeding from the puncture of nails; angels alongside angels.

On another day, I move through more halls of serene illumination in the Met. I stand in front of a marble woman who slouches in her stone chair, the folds of her dress draped heavy on her legs. It's the poet Sappho, carved in a moment of thought. Or perhaps she is composing something that centuries later will exist only as fragments, chipped pieces of language.

The more I look, the more splintered my seeing becomes. There is too much to let inside of me.

On the crowded rooftop of the museum, I start to feel dizzy. Around me, people are drinking cocktails or stretching out their arms, their cell-phones held far from their bodies to take self-portraits in the pointed light.

Years ago, I felt a similar kind of vertigo. For twelve months I was dizzy in my life. My husband had become forgetful. For a while, he forgot his love for me, left it the way he might leave his wallet in a taxicab. I, in turn, misplaced my love for him. I let it slip from my grasp, as if love were a ticket dropped somewhere on the sidewalk.

And then, one afternoon, we were driving on the highway. A song we once thought belonged to us came on the radio. My husband reached out, not to hold my hand but to turn the volume down. A decade before, he explained, when he'd been in Officer Candidate School down in Pensacola, he used to have a routine. On nights when he was permitted to leave the base, he would buy a hamburger and fries and drive his truck almost to the edge of the water and listen to this same song over and over again, thinking about me, the woman he'd dated in college. When the moon was full, hanging low on the horizon, "I thought of you," he said, because I had always called this sort of golden brightness *my moon*. When there was a storm, the lightning a jagged crack in the sky, he thought of my fear of rough weather. The song kept playing. "I thought of you," he repeated. All those years ago, he sat in the wet Florida heat, not knowing if he would see me again.

Hearing my husband remember that time, I recalled those same years, how alone I had felt, still living in the tiny apartment we once shared, with its tilted floors and windows that leaked in the rain. Late at night, ambulances sirened with their purpling lights past the building, on their way to the hospital down the street. He had left me, first for another woman and then for a career in the military. But to learn that he had been thinking about me when I was thinking of him, that he was miserable when I was miserable—to learn this changed something.

I decided to love him again.

And now I am spiraling upward into the Guggenheim, as though I am moving through the sloped structure of a nautilus, the Fibonacci shape of a white shell. I stop to visit a small exhibit of photographs before moving on to the room where a few sculptures are on display. Although I admire the oversized wood forms, hewn to resemble bodies or grave markers, it's the streamlined masses of gray-veined marble that I keep circling back to view. One looks like a spinning top. Or, from a different angle, like an ancient stone knife. Another, like a seal perched on a rock at the edge of the sea.

And always more turning, more clicking.

I have brought with me to New York several books with the word "beauty" on their covers. In Crispin Sartwell's *Six Names of Beauty*, the philosopher attempts to divide the beautiful into six categories: English, Hebrew, Sanskrit, Greek, Japanese, Navajo. I'm not sure about the endeavor in general, but I do agree with this: "The beautiful thing is not the retinal image of the sunset or the firing of neurons in the brain in response to that image, or even exactly the transport of the soul that is induced . . . We give beauty to objects and they give beauty to us; beauty is something that we make in cooperation with the world." As I walk around a marble sculpture of a woman resting her head against her hand, I look at her many sides, her cheekbones and chin. I think about my own skull in relation to hers, the pressure of the air between us, how we give ourselves to one another.

In a second book, Roger Scruton's *Beauty: A Very Short Introduction*, the author begins by arguing that "[b]eauty can be consoling, disturbing, sacred, profane; it can be exhilarating, appealing, inspiring, chilling. It can affect us in an unlimited variety of ways. Yet, it is never viewed with indifference: beauty demands to be noticed; it speaks to us directly like the voice of an intimate friend." And, yes, the marble woman with her head on her hand does speak to me. Although her eyes have been left uncarved, her mouth barely more than a notch in the stone, I can her read her expression the way I might my husband's—that is the intimacy I feel in her presence.

The third book is Elaine Scarry's *On Beauty and Being Just*. A man gave me this copy twenty years ago (perhaps as an act of courtship, his way of saying we were *true minds*). I've read it so often that it has become my primary text for thinking and speaking about the beautiful. "Beauty," Scarry tells us, "seems to incite, even require, the act of replication." I have written about this assertion before, in explaining my love of scent: "Because it is beautiful (even when ugly), perfume incites in me the act of replication. I smell that famous fragrance from the 1920s—bergamot, leather, vanilla, powder—and search for its duplicate in words." And, here in the Guggenheim, I want to make a copy of the marble woman. On the page, her cool surfaces could be touched forever by my adoring gaze.

It's only after I move downward through the museum that I come back to my own body. My feet hurt. I'm thirsty. I need to sit outside and empty myself of so many images. In the 1800s, during his travels through Italy, Stendahl wrote about this same experience of being overwhelmed by art:

My soul, affected by the very notion of being in Florence, and by the proximity of those great men whose tombs I had just beheld, was already in a state of trance . . . As I emerged from the porch of *Santa Croce*, I was seized with a fierce palpitation of the heart (that same symptom which, in Berlin, is referred to as an *attack of nerves*); the well-spring of life was dried up within me, and I walked in constant fear of falling to the ground.

We call this Stendahl syndrome. Today, I feel as I do when I've been in a department store, after having smelled too many perfumes. A sales associate might try to hand me a small glass filled with coffee beans. I am told that the scent will *clear* my nose and allow me to sniff again. It's nonsense, of course. Once the nose is full of clashing aromas, the only solution is to wait until the air empties itself of fragrance. Seeing those pictures, being filled with their clamorous beauties, all I can do is swoon. I wait until my eyes can see again, the mind able to regard each separate object in its own frame.

Later, when I scroll through the photographs on my phone, I only find a portion of the beauty I observed at the museums. In my photographs, only the act of aiming the camera remains. What's missing is the body breathing rapidly or holding its breath in proximity to the art.

Where has the rest gone?

Standing outside the Guggenheim, I remember again that afternoon, long ago, when I first decided to love my husband again. In falling out of love with him—not once, but now twice in our marriage, maybe more, if I'm honest with myself—I have become like one of those museumgoers who holds her cell phone out in front of her, the device a small barrier to keep the canvas's immersive colors at a distance.

If love, too, is a kind of syndrome, I am unswooning in my husband's presence, no longer subject to a "fierce palpitation of the heart." I don't just mean desire can fade. I mean that marriage is like a gallery where the lighting is too bright, and all we can do is keep studying the small flaws in the paintings. Marriage is the courtyard that looks like a cohesive whole until we move closer and discover that the pillars have disparate origins, are a persuasive collage of relics.

The books I have carried with me to New York say, "beauty is some-thing that we make in cooperation with the world," that "beauty demands to be noticed," that beauty "seems to incite, even require, the act of repli-cation." But it does something else, too. It takes a seat inside us and, in the process, nudges us a little beyond our own comfort. It's the guest who makes himself at home; he scatters his belongings around the spare bed-room, crumpled clothes left on a chair, a suitcase sitting open on the floor, some toiletries uncapped on the nightstand. He stays too long, so that we end up saying to the visitor, *I'm just going out for a short walk*, in order to find a moment of quiet again.

The tourists in the museums are holding their cell phones in front of them because they don't want to invite the guest of beauty inside. Click. Turn. Click. Turn.

My husband, too, is a lodger who has made his home in me. And whenever I choose not to love him, it's because I feel that love, like beauty, disrupts my silent hours.

Lodge, both the noun and the verb, contains a threat. Yes, according to the *OED*, the word means "small house or dwelling." But it is also "a place of confinement; a cell, prison." It is "to succeed in causing (a weapon, a blow) to fall and take effect where it is aimed." A lodger isn't merely one who "resides" but archaically, too, is "one who sleeps or passes the night in a place." The lodger visits, then leaves.

One of the real threats of beauty—and, for that matter, of love—is not that it comes to reside inside me, but that its stay could be temporary. On any day, I might look at a photograph of a golden object behind glass and feel its loss, how the gleaming is suddenly unremarkable, my turning and clicking having possessed nothing.

When I leave New York and go home, perhaps I will look at the man curled beside me in bed and continue to wonder, *where is it going, where has it gone—my love for him?*

Back home, I will hear him breathing slowly in the almost-dark. The safe gesture will be this: to lie down, to move to the edge of the mattress, so that my back faces his. There will be distance between us, the blankets a woolen boundary. The riskier motion is this: to lay my pillow alongside his, watching the stone outline of his nose and mouth or listening to the tender, vulnerable sound his body makes when he's deepest asleep. I will reach out to touch the sheet draped like a piece of carved marble across him. And even if, in dreaming, he rolls away from me, leaving no part of him to touch, I will keep my hand on the warm place he leaves behind.

Snapshot / Dallas, 2022

[Even when the arm is naked, my skin appears patterned as if by cloth. I wear a covert of flowers, a scavenger bird perched in blue shadow, the face of a woman in silhouette. The work took many hours. I lay still on a table so that the needle could pen its permanent marks in me. There were weeks of healing, the design raised like a thin thread I could follow with my fingertips. For almost a year after, I hid the ink beneath fabric, sleeve beneath sleeve, afraid to show how sharp the claws of the grackle at my wrist. At each appointment, the artist said I was a "good surface"—I take the ink so well it barely fades. I take the ink as though I were thick paper unrolled to the length of a body and flattened with a weight.]

GALLERY FOUR

Ambivalent Things

Kiddush Cup

It sits on a high shelf. The cup is positioned among the other pieces of Judaica I have bought over the last two decades. It is tulip-shaped, as if belief were a flower I might drink from.

I like to look at the cup and its companions. I didn't grow up in a house with a collection of antique silver displayed on the dining room credenza. No pieces tarnished sepia-brown. No candlesticks and platters smuggled from Europe during the long years of extermination. Instead, there were towers of mid-century porcelain plates, crystal vases bought tax-free in airport gift shops, tchotchkes my parents picked up during their years posted overseas. In the 1930s, their parents entered the United States as refugees with almost nothing. And in the decades after they became Americans, all four of my grandparents acquired possessions that had no provenance.

I'm reminded of a passage from Daniel Mendelsohn's *The Lost*, a memoir in which the author attempts to uncover how six of his relatives were murdered in the Shoah. Mendelsohn frequently brings his training as a classicist to his search for the dead, as when he recounts a moment from *The Aeneid* to explain what he calls "the poignantly unbridgeable distances created by time." Aeneas and his companion arrive in Carthage and walk through the town:

What does the writer know about belief? In this opening passage we see that, yes, she trusts her eyes. She has faith in the weight of the cup in her hand or the hardness of its lip when placed to her own lips. But she can't remember the last time she filled the cup with wine or recited the usual blessing to sanctify the Sabbath—in English, of course, because the only Hebrew she can read is a transliteration. *Baruch atah, Adonai Eloheinu, Melech haolam, borei p'ri hagafen.* If she sounds out the words carefully, we might almost suppose these words come from knowledge.

A reader might wonder: why keep a cup from which she hardly drinks? We should understand that even secular families own pieces of Judaica. These things are reminders of pain that refused to stay buried, the Shoah continuing to unearth itself across Europe. Somewhere in Poland, a set of silver Torah finials are found beneath the floorboards of a former synagogue. Every year, a dented Kiddush cup is discovered in a Ukrainian field. The ground is constantly offering up sacred books, dishes to serve honey in the New Year, even a gold stylus sculpted to look like a pointing finger.

Suddenly, in a magnificent new temple, the two men stop dead in their tracks in front of a mural that is decorated with pictures of the Trojan War. For the Carthaginians, the war is just a decorative motif, something to adorn the walls of their new temple; for Aeneas, of course, it means much more, and as he stands looking at this picture, which is the picture of his life, he bursts into tears and utters a tormented line of Latin . . . *sunt lacrimae rerum*, "There are tears in things."

No tears fill the author's Kiddush cup. After her wedding day, this goblet was used only once, for a Shabbat dinner a decade ago. We conjuncture that if she were to fill the cup to the rim with wine and drink from it, the liquid would likely taste of itself or of new metal, that unmistakable sharpness that resembles the tang of blood.

There is an obscure story about the author. She once recited the Mourner's Kaddish at her Oma's funeral. *Yitgadal v'yitkadash sh'mei raba.* When she read the phrases transliterated from the Aramaic, the sounds felt briefly familiar in her mouth, as if grief could teach a language her ancestors spoke. As she stared at the sheet of plastic grass that had been laid around her grandmother's coffin to hide the open hole and the wet, fresh dirt, she realized she was swaying back and forth, suddenly pious, if only for the few minutes of prayer. What can we make of this wavering in the body? Scholars have yet to agree. We do not know why the Kaddish can move even those unmoved by the idea of a power beyond and above.

When I look at the Kiddush cup, I feel the unbridgeable distance, not so much between the vessel and me, but between who I am and the Jews who prayed with all sincerity, somewhere in my family's past. Every week they bowed their heads and said the blessing over the cup to mark the start of Shabbat. They followed strictly the 613 mitzvot prescribed by the Torah, their bodies and days governed by intricate laws.

Shabbat Candlesticks

We keep the burning in ourselves.
    We're paired: one of us made

to remember, and the other to observe.
    Some nights we grasp the glow forever,

each wick a disappearance of the day.
    Dripping wax resembles tears.

But soon it hardens to the faint
    translucence of a piece of stone, marble

carved to look like something liquid.
   We hold you to your word,

that every week contains a small apportioning
   of joy. We never leave you

sitting in the dark. You strike the match—
   we lift the tender flames.

Mezuzah Case

There's a company in Poland that sells mezuzah cases made from the impressions left on the doorways of Jewish houses. First, the company creates an imprint of the spot where the original mezuzah case was once nailed. At the foundry, a mold is then made from that impression and filled with molten bronze. Later, it's polished, the edges rubbed to smoothness, and the case engraved with the Hebrew letter Shin, which stands for the word *Shaddai*, one of the names for God.

On the computer screen, the mezuzot are stout rectangles, ugly but well-made. They retain the texture of wood, stone, or brick. For $240, customers can buy the gleaming impression of a mezuzah that once hung near the entry of a building in Kraków, Warsaw, or even Kielce—the site of a vicious pogrom in 1946 that killed forty-two Jews and hurt forty others, in a fury of gunshots and the jab of bayonets.

These cases are fashioned out of absence, uncanny inversions of the past. They are ghost mezuzot, miniature caskets.

For $40 more, one can order a kosher scroll known as a klaf. When rolled, the piece of parchment is small enough to fit inside the case. Every case needs a klaf. Without the holy words handwritten by a scribe, the mezuzah is only a container holding nothing but a tiny pocket of dark air.

Imagine the candlesticks on the shelf could speak. They would say the author is good at remembering. But observing Shabbat? Well, not so much. Here is a story the author has omitted from the text. When her father was twelve years old and studying for his bar mitzvah, each time he made a mistake with the cantillation, the uneasy chant of the Torah, the rabbi would press a sharpened pencil point into the boy's palm. By the end of each practice, her father's hand was inscribed with a precise and pulsing wound. This was his earliest lesson about religion, that it is cruel, that it leaves a painful mark. He bequeathed this memory to his daughter. *Please, take this,* he said.

The author owns a mezuzah, too. It was not made from the impression of a phantom case. Instead, it is new and American, a silver branch adorned with a metal orchid, so detailed that the flower seems about to bloom. We should note the author has never removed the mezuzah from the cardboard box in which it came. Like other scholars, we interpret this fact as evidence she's too afraid to affix it by her front door. Better, she thinks, in a world of synagogue shootings and new blood libels, if her neighbors don't discover they're living near a Jew.

Challah Cover

Once there was a baker renowned in the village for her breads. Some she scattered with rye, as if the loaves were open fields that needed planting. Some she knotted into rolls. And a few she braided like a girl's fine hair.

In the late mornings, after she laid her goods on long, wooden trays, the people came as though they were starving birds. Even while the breads were still warm, they tore through the crusts, eating straight to the center, like rabbits burrowing in a hole. The woman loved her work, but she hated to see the food treated with such hurry; we are commanded, she knew, to savor every bite. And so she thought to conceal her most treasured breads, at least until they had time to cool and the sun was lowering beyond the trees, the way a bubbe might lower herself slowly onto a kitchen stool. After a few days, the baker had an idea. She pulled on a little thread of moonlight. She stitched a cover that gleamed with early evening. Every Friday after that, she placed two braided loaves beneath the piece of fabric she had sewn, as if tucking two children into bed. In this way, she made sure there was always enough bread saved for the Sabbath, the sweetness of challah sprinkled with salt, a small reminder of the possibility of tears, even in the times when we are blessed.

Never mind the other stories you might have heard about breads and why we guard them. On this matter, I swear by the trout that swim in the Vistula River. I have heard the truth from the baker herself.

Ketubah

Dearest, I betroth you to me for as long as we can stand the other's breathing. I will take the garbage out on Wednesday nights. I will make you pancakes on Sunday mornings. Set me as a pillow beneath your heart, for love should be a

An enticing tale, yes? The author is skilled at mimicking the voices of writers like I. B. Singer and Sholem Aleichem, although she knows no Yiddish. She once received a recipe for challah from a family friend whose kitchen contains two stoves, two sinks, meat and dairy kept separate as strangers. As for the author, she has never baked a single loaf. She doesn't want to give the long hours required of this art, the knead and the rise, the brush of egg white on the dough. She cannot show such devotion to the braided bread, which is not so much food but a commandment or a symbol of the miraculous. And the silk challah cover that the author bought years ago—appliquéd with the luminous shapes of fruit—remains folded in a drawer.

cushioned place to rest. And I will laugh when you laugh, will be quiet when you're reading, will bring you a blanket when the room goes cold. I will respect the unruly coiling of your hair. I will understand that sometimes you want to be alone. May I like you even before your first cup of coffee, when the sleep is still crusted in your eyes. May our hearts be joined by the small arguments. Let our home be modest enough that we cannot hide ourselves in distant rooms. When we have offered jagged words, let our home be rich with making up and making up again.

Seder Plate

First there are bitter herbs.

And then there are more bitter herbs, this history a long list of bitterness that never leaves the mouth.

Next there is a shankbone cleaned of meat. Remember the blood on the lintel and death winging over in the night.

There is a vegetable that might mean hope is a green tendril growing from the earth. Don't forget to dip it in the little bowl of weeping.

There is a paste of apple, nuts, and cinnamon, sweet though it represents the memory of enslavement, the mortar used to build the Pyramids.

And last, a roasted egg. Some say it's for the sacrifice in the temple. Some say it's for mourning that refuses to end.

Yes, there are cups of wine. There's unrisen bread. There's a plate of food for the prophet who might never arrive.

Menorah

When I was a child, my parents had a menorah, which they displayed occasionally during the eight nights of Chanukah. It was made of iron nails welded together with bright

Long before she wrote this essay, the author searched for a ketubah with the most progressive language she could find. Her future husband was a lapsed Catholic, and she was a Jew who struggled against tradition, how it constricted like the boning in a wedding dress. The ketubah they chose is a liquid field of yellow floating above a plain of purple; it could have been a painting by Mark Rothko, a nonbeliever too whose thinking was also deeply Jewish. The text they selected avoids the Orthodox avowals of virgins and silver zuzim. Nonetheless, she even resisted the *lets* and *mays* of the ketubah they finally settled on, phrases borrowed from the Song of Songs, the milder imperatives of the contract to which she signed her name.

Scholars have observed that, of all the Jewish holidays, Pesach is the one toward which the author feels the least resistance. Perhaps it is because Passover recounts the passing on of pain. Moses negotiates freedom for his people by wounding Pharaoh, because sometimes the only answer to a wound is to wound the wounder tenfold. This author appears to understand, even if a man like Moses—someone called by God as the desert bramble bursts into flames—mostly resists her comprehension. When Moses and his people finally escape across the torn seam of the Red Sea, they remain stitched to their old suffering, uncertain of their God. They are lost in the wilderness of their trauma for forty years. As for the Seder plate in the author's house, it has six concavities, each one shaped like a pomegranate. Maybe belief isn't a flower but a piece of fruit dangling from a branch. We might say she's not standing too far below to reach it. She has simply never wanted to stretch her arm toward something so equally astringent and sweet.

drips of brass to form each stem, a Brutalist design, hard and modern.

I would sit before the unlighted menorah, my chin resting on my hands, and stare for many minutes at its outline. Occasionally, I pressed a finger against one of the iron nails. The metal tip had been smoothed out but, if I had pushed hard enough, I could have broken my skin.

In an essay titled "Thing Theory," scholar Bill Brown explores what he calls "the thingness of objects."

> As they circulate through our lives, we look through objects . . . but we only catch a glimpse of things. We look through objects because there are codes by which our interpretive attention makes them meaningful, because there is a discourse of objectivity that allows us to use them as facts. A thing, in contrast, can hardly function as a window. We begin to confront the thingness of objects when they stop working for us: when the drill breaks, when the car stalls, when the windows get filthy, when their flow within the circuits of production and distribution, consumption and exhibition, has been arrested, however momentarily.

The Kiddush cup and the challah cover and the Seder plate are full of their own thingness. They have stopped working for me. No, that's not right. I have never allowed them to work, never asked that they function as more than the kind of decorative motifs that once made Aeneas weep in Carthage. I have only looked at them, never through.

These things are meant to come after the idea of belief. They are supposed to concretize faith. If that devotion doesn't exist, then the cup and the cover and plate can still be touched. But do they weigh an ounce less? Do they shimmer less? Delight less?

Consider how this menorah evokes the word *stigma*, from the Greek meaning "mark of a pointed instrument, puncture, tattoo-mark, brand." In another religion, stigmata are a body's evidence of devotion. To own such a menorah, iconography of torture and redemption, a savior rising from the dead . . . we wonder what the author's parents felt in selecting this thing for their home. Maybe the choice was aesthetic; they liked its barbed silhouette. Maybe they wished, in some way, to belong to a later faith, one demanding love instead of the old obedience, to a different god perhaps, who didn't command "Take now thy son, thine only son Isaac," Mount Moriah a grim shadow in the distance. Or maybe they understood that Judaism is a religion of sharp questions. Scholars write commentary in the margins, accumulating centuries of inquiry and argument.

I didn't know the word *ambivalence* when I was small. If I had, I would have pointed to the menorah of nails and named it my family's ambivalence. We were Jews without belief, but still believed ourselves Jews, angry at a God whose presence we doubted, our faith abandoned a generation ago, in the ghettos or at the border crossings of another continent. This menorah seemed to say, belief is rigid and piercing. It will hurt you to believe.

But we might reach a different conclusion here. We say she is the cup waiting to be filled. She is also the empty case and the bread uncovered. Used or not, a thing of the old world or the new, she too is made to hold the burning, to lift the light with her soldered spikes.

GALLERY FIVE

Jewel Box

Anyone, with enough new yards of fabric, can stitch a quilt. It's easy to cut the bolts into strips, the blade rolling against the ruler, each inch of cloth identical and straight. Even a beginner can drag the unvarying lengths through the sewing machine.

But leftover scraps, you remind yourself, are small and shaped unevenly; they require more skill to piece. You find instructions for a block called Jewel Box. There are pairs of triangles joined, squares the size of postage stamps.

The design is known as Jewel Box because, when you place the blocks side by side, dozens of diamonds emerge, faceted and glittering, in a field of smaller gems.

There's pleasure in standing back to survey your handiwork. You like ordering the mess into something warm. Others mistake this art for softness, all fluffy batting and the stitching together of layers, the intimacy of what covers the world of the bed, desire and dreaming, the deep, heavy fever, even the nights when the body refuses to sleep.

This art isn't soft. It's the imposition of your will on cotton scraps. You suffer the pinprick and the thread that snarls the machine. Your scissors are sharp. You snip. You hold the steel needle. You make the iron's steaming kiss.

Dear Rose

Whatever I imagined, my grandmother could render in fabric. We often began by flipping through the pages of fashion magazines, making note of necklines we liked, the shape of sleeves, the artful positioning of darts. Oma bent close to look at the pictures, nodded at what she saw. She might point to a photograph and describe something she'd sewn forty years before in Germany. "But not so long a skirt," she might say, "not so pleated like this." Then I sketched a design in my favorite notebook, the one with the dense, textured paper that made me feel like a grown-up designer. We discussed color, whether the fabric should be cut on the bias, what sort of closures down the back.

She took my measurements quickly, writing each one—neck, shoulder to shoulder, bust, upper arm, wrist, waist, hips—on a little sheet of paper, her cursive knotted and indecipherable, in the way of handwriting learned long ago and in another country.

❧

At the Dallas Museum of Art, I walk through *Dior: From Paris to the World*, an exhibition of seventy years' worth of garments produced by the fashion house that Christian Dior founded in 1947. As my silver guidebook proclaims, Dior's "vision of clothing based on strong, architectural lines resonated in a world rebuilding itself from the ground up after the devastation of World War II." The designer's most famous dresses transformed woman's bodies from "the boxy, masculine silhouettes of wartime fashion" into a series of curves, "with rounded shoulders, a generous bust, a tiny waist, and accentuated hips." These proportions—the wasp waist, the flair of a full skirt below—came to be known as the New Look, a shape that turned women into elegant flowers perched on satin pumps.

The first room in the exhibition is tiered, its acrylic floors red as the glossy polish on the fingernails of a woman of leisure. All the clothing here is black: black gowns and suits, black for all times of the day. I wonder if, in a world immediately after war, even the most glamorous women of Paris felt they should dress as though for mourning. A wide black skirt topped with a white jacket stands out from the rest. "[A]fternoon ensemble in silk shantung and pleated wool." The moonglow gleam of the jacket couldn't be any more fitted on the mannequin's torso. The excellence of this tailoring is evident, the knowledge it took to shape fabric like a glistening skin, folded and moving against the body, but also tight along the chest, barely enough space for breath.

ເ∕ວ

Dear Rose, I have been teaching myself to weave. It's not that I dislike the sewing machine, but I want a discipline of my own, for my fingers to learn another art. I think you would have liked the language of this craft: the heddle, the reed, the shuttle, the hook, the paw, the peg, the warp, the weft, the shed.

These are solid words. They seem to have existed since the beginning of speech, like "bread" or "dirt" or "blood." I say them, and I feel their comforting, stable shapes in my mouth.

So much is unraveling in this America you once made your home.

The loom is light enough to sit on my lap or fit in a canvas bag for carrying. To warp it, I clip the loom to a tabletop, using a hook to thread yarn through the long slats of the reed. Sixty times, the yarn is looped around the peg. When I wind the warp, there is a clicking sound. And then, the slowest work: to thread every other strand of yarn through the tiny eyes. Finally, I pull them taut and tie them off in bunches.

I want to form something usable with my hands. I want to control its length and width, determine its colors, how sturdy or delicate it will be, what purpose it will serve.

Because she was born in 1909 and grew up in Stuttgart during WWI and the Depression, Oma was thrifty. She cut her patterns from old grocery bags, smoothing out the wrinkled brown paper on a table. She didn't need store-bought patterns like McCall's or Butterick. She could glance at any garment and recognize its individual parts: for instance, how the sleeves might notch into the bodice, or the way the waist attached to the skirt, and in what order these steps had occurred.

Every movement was decisive, her fingers confident alongside the stabbing hum of the sewing machine's needle, feeding the fabric through. She worked as much by sound as by sight, listening for a catch of the thread, a hesitation in the engine, her slippered foot attentive on the pedal. When hand-stitching, she leaned toward the strip of cloth in front of her, her glasses sliding to the tip of her nose, the thimble a silvered extension of her finger. I learned, early on, that this is what expertise looks like. This was the certainty of a body that—for decades—had apprenticed itself to one art. How excellent it felt to watch someone who was excellent at what she did, every gesture the result of hundreds of hours of training.

✧

Another room, titled the "Office of Dreams," presents the viewer with rows of white dresses and jackets. These are known as toiles, sample garments sewn in pale muslin, what my brochure describes as "mock-ups." Floating on the bleached bodies of mannequins, they are like apparitions of the clothing to come.

✧

I am weaving enough fabric to make a coat, dear Rose. The inches happen slowly, and I will need many yards to form the sleeve, the placket, the back, the two flaps at the front. But, one day, I will be kept warm with a thing of my own doing.

I think you would understand: when I am weaving, I exist in a space where there is nothing but the clack, clack, clack. No borders of countries to be crossed. No tyrant signing orders with the thick swoop of a pen. There is only the stop when the shuttle gets stuck in the shed, catching the warp. The faint pull of strands tightening against the wood. The ball of yarn bouncing across the ground. The little nudge of my dog's nose as she pushes the skein beneath the couch.

❧

For my twelfth birthday, Oma and I visited a Washington, DC, landmark, G Street Fabrics, three stories of cottons, velvets, and silks. I had decided my newest dress would contain as much pink as we could fit into a single piece of clothing: pink moiré silk, its surface glistening like water, pink lace at the neck, pink pearls down the front, a pink bow in my hair, another tied at my waist. We wandered the rows of the store, our fingers sliding up and down across the rounded bolts, pausing to feel to the slip of satin, the rough nubble of wool. "Oma," I would say to her, "touch this." Or she would call to me, "Puppele," little doll, "come, see—what good chiffon."

Within a day, I saw that the real dress was even better than the fantasy sketch in my notebook, pink against pink, each ripple and crease set deliberately against my form. This is what clothing became for me: a dream made real and wearable, perfectly constructed by someone who loved me, who loved how a dress can transform the body, the clothing we put on a way of stepping into our own futures.

Later, as an adult, I learned clothing could be something else as well: a thing that damages bodies and soil and air. It could be the Triangle Shirt-waist Factory fire in New York. "One hundred and forty-six died in the flames / On the ninth floor, no hydrants, no fire escapes," writes Robert Pinsky, in his poem "Shirt." It could be other blazes in Lahore and Karachi. It could be the collapse of the Rana Plaza building in Dhaka.

And what about the hands that snipped loose threads from the collar of my store-bought blouse? Were they the size and dexterity of my grand-mother's? Some days, I clipped the price tag from a dress and wondered what the fabric would look like in ten or twenty washes. Would the first stain be oil or wine? How long before this piece ended in a landfill, surrounded by millions of other garments?

That clothing can be ethical or unethical, sustainable or not—Oma taught me that a part of the maker is sewn into every seam, the soreness of her fingers, the blurred exhaustion of her eyes, the acute angle of her back. "The label," Pinsky says, but also "the labor, the color, the shade. The shirt."

∾

What questions are raised by the things produced in Dior's ateliers? Here's a "[g]ala dress in tulle embroidered with sequins and beads," its gauzy surface the color of ripe raspberries, glistening with ruddy pearls and other red-dipped accents. I circle the gown, trying to picture the hands that made it, how many hours it took to fill the bodice with ornamentation, the intimacy required to hold such delicate mesh and fix it in place.

∾

Rose, on days when the news talks on and on, I am anxious at the loom. I feel the unspooling yarn. The diminishing weight of the shuttle. The sticky threads of the warp. The looping back. The press of the batten or beater. The tension that snaps. The fray. The pull. The cut end.

∾

My conversations with Oma were most often about clothing and Germany: the many thicknesses of wool, what she remembered of the country, tricks for finishing off a buttonhole, what she carried with her when she left in 1936. In my memories of our long afternoons, clothing and Germany seemed stitched together, like the two threads of a sewing machine, the one fed from the spool pin at the top and the other pulled from the bobbin underneath.

The first story I remember her telling me was about her father's death. It was Passover, and the whole family came down with food poisoning. Her father was so sick they took him to the hospital, but none of the doctors would treat a Jew. Shortly after he died, two members of the S.S. arrived at the house looking for my great-grandfather. My great-grandmother, a burning temper of a redhead, said, "You're looking for my husband? I'll take you to him." She walked with the officers to the cemetery. Reaching his burial plot, she pointed to the fresh mound of dirt.

"There he is," she said. "You can have him."

No doubt we were holding fabric when Oma presented this dark swatch of our family's story. Maybe we were basting a hem or stitching a hook and eye to the closure of a neck. I learned how to manage a needle by the time I was three or four, my fingers gifted in these tiny tasks. And I loved listening to Oma's voice as we laid out pattern pieces on the dining room table, how sometimes she would slip into a few words of her native German or the Spanish she learned when the family fled finally to Honduras.

✌

Next, I stand in front of what's described simply as a "[p]rinted taffeta evening gown," designed by Yves Saint Laurent in 1960. I know Oma would have loved its asymmetrical hemline, the dramatic bow drooping above the bell-shaped skirt, the stiff fabric painted with red and black flowers.

I never saw my grandmother wearing a dress like this, although she certainly sewed elaborate ensembles for my mother. When my parents were married at New York City Hall, Mommy—who had the face of a 1940s movie star and whose figure nipped to a tiny circumference at the waist—wore turquoise silk that rippled when she moved. As a child, I often opened the drawer where she stored the dress, touching the seawater shimmer of the fabric, circling my finger around the perimeter of each pearl button.

✌

When I make a mistake on the loom, Rose, I retrace the movements of my hands to undo the error, the shuttle sent backward through the shed, which is that open area made by the alternating strands of the warp, half angled up and half down. The shuttle travels in reverse, and when it reaches the end, I shift the heddle into its other position, creating a new shed, now half of the warp slanting down and half up. I travel backward and back, until I find the site of my blunder and erase it. Could a country do this, I wonder, undo its own tangles in the textile? Yes, I think, a country might unravel itself, disappear its history, so that what's left is only the sheen of cloth.

Then I begin to advance again, the fabric on the loom lengthening.

☙

It was my grandmother who persuaded much of the family to leave Germany in 1936. By that point, the government had denied her permission to accept a scholarship to study haute couture in Paris. She was working in an atelier in Stuttgart. The woman who ran the studio liked my grandmother's swift, careful hands. Still, despite her skill with a needle, Oma—alone, of all the employees, the only Jew—was often seated in the darkest corner of the room, so that she struggled with the fine stitches and delicate beadwork.

Under these conditions, Oma began to consider setting up her own dress shop. But, she realized, while a few gentile clients might be willing to come to her in the secret hours of evening or early morning, most would be too afraid to break the national boycott of Jewish businesses. *Kauft nicht bei Juden!* read the signs and posters.

She was 27 years old. The family had relatives who had settled in San Pedro Sula many decades before. Thank God, it wasn't too late to get out.

☙

In a grand, vaulted hall there are dozens of dresses on display. They have names like Mimi-San, Bosphore, Byzance, Bengale, and Kigely. "For Dior's successors," the exhibit brochure explains, "world art and cultures have been endless sources of inspiration." Rick Brettel of the *Dallas Morning News* frames this portion of the exhibit in a more complex way: "With geographically and culturally diverse sources from Maasai warriors to Japanese geisha, these costumes have a Euro-colonialist quality. As much as they celebrate the diverse 'inspiration' of Dior's designers, they also left me feeling uncomfortable about the global ambitions of the house." The problem is that here cultural and religious traditions of dressing have been stripped of context, reduced to mere ornamentation. In this great hall, a kimono is no longer worn to mark mourning or celebration, for instance, but is simply a distinctive silhouette adorned with a luxury of pink blossoms. An Al Amira is now an opportunity for beading, the decorative motif of a tiger skin spreading across a veil that is meant to indicate modesty. A deity from ancient Egyptian iconography, bird-headed and gleaming, is now a mannequin wearing a gold lamé column dress embroidered with blue lotuses.

Appealing to the eye, yes. But even beautiful clothing cannot be unknotted from place or history. What did Christian Dior do during WWII? My exhibition guidebook calls that time "the dark years." Of course, there's more to the story. As Brettel points out, "Dior's years of apprenticeship were of crucial importance to his career. He started in the house of Robert Piguet, where he worked with Pierre Balmain and Marc Bohan before serving in the French military. After early release from the military, Dior worked in the house of Lucien Lelong, where, like other designers, he survived by designing dresses for the wives of Nazi officers and their French collaborators." Depending on which sources I consult, Dior and other French designers of the era are represented either as traitors or as patriots, either sewing elegant apparel for the occupiers or else working to save the Parisian fashion industry from the Nazis who aspired to make Berlin a new center of haute couture.

Decades later, John Galliano was fired from his role as creative director of Dior after being arrested in Paris for shouting antisemitic slurs. On a video, he was shown saying, "'I love Hitler, and people like you would be dead today. Your mothers, your forefathers, would be all be gassed and dead." In a *New York Times* report of the incident, Galliano is characterized as "one of the great fashion talents of the last 20 years, known for his imagination and nearly unmatched technical skills." And, according to my brochure, Galliano, who worked for Dior from 1997 to 2011, departed from the firm "amid controversy."

I suppose the message here is that high fashion can place a silky gauze over the bruised skin of history. Look how history becomes elegant when draped in textiles that reflect the light. Look at the figure of history, its small waist, balanced by bust and hips, how graceful the leg.

☙

And, Rose, there is a final transformation that a woven textile undergoes. After removing the cloth from the loom, I submerge it in water. Then I agitate it, rubbing the fabric against itself, squeezing its fibers, until the separate strands bind together, cohesive and strong. This process is called wet-finishing. Once the textile dries, it is stronger than before, its threads now supple, bending with the body that wears it.

The metaphor is plain: to be submerged, to be agitated, to be made more resilient. I'm not weaving democracy a winding sheet. If anything, I'm inventing the fabric that, in my imagination, you might have wrapped around your body. It would be a fine, strong suit of blue-checked wool, flecks of purple in the weft, sturdy enough to wear when marching on a street or lifting a sign in the air.

☙

If I want to, I can—for a while—mend my grandmother's story, make a version in which there never were Nazis. I can undo the weaving so that there were no Nuremberg Laws, my great-grandfather not dead from bad fish and the indifference of racist doctors. Oma was never prevented from moving to Paris. There never was a Second World War, no Vichy regime that might have imprisoned her in Drancy and then sent her to Auschwitz, had she ever arrived in France. There never was a need for reparations by the German government in an aftermath that wasn't. And by the late 1940s, she might have been working in the atelier of the newly formed fashion house run by Christian Dior, a man who didn't sew gowns for the wives of German officers. Oma might have become a première, supervising a staff of more than twenty, a woman known for her rigorous standards, the precision of her work. After some years, she might have started her own line, naming it after herself, *Rose*, a tiny rosebud on the tag of every dress.

At the exhibition, when I bend down to study the glass case of embroidery and beadwork, I can imagine my grandmother's hands working this fabric, the way she would have used the point of her needle to pick up each crystal and rondelle from the tray before her, each brass sequin.

Or, in a room labeled "Fields of Flowers," I stand before a ball gown of pale green tulle and, beneath the mesh layers, dozens of red silk poppies. Of course, the dress looks like an Impressionist painting given body, a scene from the rainbowed gardens at Giverny. But it's also a garment of sadness. Blossoms of the silent country. Blossoms of trauma. Blossoms of remembrance. I can imagine my grandmother's hands here as well. She is stitching the dimensional flowers into the lake of this dress, her hands here forever, petals sinking and then floating in the mossy surface of the water.

Snapshots / Denton, 2018

[Right now, I'm living decades ago, which is to say the spiced cookie I eat this afternoon returns me to West Berlin when I was fifteen. In a gold and marble Konditorei, my father ordered cups of coffee. I drank black tea. The lebkuchen tasted so sweet, it was easy to forget we were sitting in a divided city.]

[A friend emails me from the Middle East to ask if we were ever forced to leave a post overseas. I write to tell her, "Yes, from Zaire, when I was three." All I remember is nothing of that departure from Lubumbashi. The evacuation was so sudden that, years later in Brussels, I would have to relearn the French I once knew as a little girl, language like crumbs brushed clean from a porcelain plate.]

[In the high-ceilinged rooms of the past, a waltz keeps playing. *Onetwothree onetwothree onetwothree.* I am eating or drinking somewhere far away.]

[A friend calls me from New York. It's midnight, and neither of us can sleep again. We can't decide which country will be first to shatter. On the other end of the line, I can hear her reheating her coffee, the small *ping* of warning from the microwave.]

["Tikkun olam," I say to her or she says to me. For Jews, it means repairing the broken world. We are always talking like this. And I'm telling her about the Poland of my childhood, the paper bags of plums, the baskets of raspberries bleeding juice, how I used to wander through Warsaw, touching the gray exteriors of buildings, feeling for the absence made by bullets, their ricochet.]

Provenance

I remember the dourness of the Viennese. Their way of speaking, a tone that turned every sentence bitter. The clean streets. The trams arriving and departing at exactly the hours listed on the timetable. The city laid out in numbered districts. The rain, the hard air even on sunlit corners. The fur collars flipped up against the wind. The cafés with their soft clicks of spoons in teacups. The muffled children. Or else the signs forbidding children in those rooms. The dogs on their tight leashes. The glass cases lined with iced and gilded shapes. The customers perfectly trained in the act of silence, the edge of every fork cutting deep into the cake.

℘

Home from college on winter break, all I wanted was a piece of Sacher Torte. At the time, my family was living in Vienna, my father having been assigned to a position at the intergovernmental organization known as the OSCE, the Operation for Security and Co-operation in Europe. We lived on a quiet residential street, the apartment a cream-colored rectangle, two stories tall, with numerous bedrooms and bathrooms, a spacious living and dining room, and a private garden off to one side.

Under different circumstances, we would have been thrilled by the generous accommodations, the apartment's high ceilings and long stretches of shined wooden floors an extravagance in such an expensive city. But this was Vienna, which meant that censure often accompanied luxury. The grim Austrian woman who lived next door frequently called the OSCE to complain about the presence of these inconvenient American diplomats.

None of us had ever met or even seen her. But we received reports of her fury. I liked to imagine her as thin, wrapped in an olive-green coat of felted wool, a dead fox biting its own tail around her neck. I was certain she must wear her gray hair in a bun so tight it pulled her face into an expression of distaste, her mouth pinched and sour, as if she had just bitten into a mealy apple.

Whatever I might have felt about the Viennese, I knew that I wanted to eat a slice of the city's famous Sacher Torte, which was the traditional cake of our family, after all. Every year, on birthdays and other special occasions, my father baked one. He used his mother's recipe; it was one of the treasures she carried with her when she escaped Europe during the Second World War. And, before she died, my grandmother gave her recipe for Sacher Torte to her son, a piece of yellowed paper folded between the pages of her favorite cookbook. The instructions were not hard to follow. He learned to replicate the dense crumb of the cake, how to spread apricot jam—thin as a windowpane—between the two layers, and across the whole surface, a glossy chocolate icing, smooth as a mirror.

❧

In Vienna, my parents spoke the German they had learned in childhood. My father grew up in Miami, in a house where the dinner table was set with Rosenthal porcelain. Every week, his mother baked cakes and layered concoctions and various kinds of cookies to feed the ladies who came over for a kaffeeklatsch, the coffee the rich, unburned brown that Berliners prefer. Like most conversations in that home, those afternoon get-togethers were conducted largely in German, every woman in the room a recent immigrant to the United States, Jewish refugees turned suddenly American, their voices still thickly accented with the intonations of the cities they had fled in the 1930s and '40s. Some of their bodies were still brittle, narrow from the war. Others were going plump, their flowered cotton dresses tight at the waist, as though they were making up for lost meals by eating every sweet or starchy thing.

My mother's German was learned in San Pedro Sula, as well as the

Spanish she spoke at the local Catholic school and the small pieces of Yiddish she practiced by reading her father's socialist newspapers. The family, blocked—like so many others—from entering the United States, had escaped to Honduras instead. My mother's German could slide easily into Spanish and, later, when her family immigrated to Florida, into English, on her tongue the movement between one language and the next smooth as melted butter.

My parents met at Coral Gables Senior High School. They were enrolled in the same advanced German class. My father's senior year, they acted opposite one another in *Der Krämerskorb* by Hans Sachs. My mother held a rolling pin. The blocking required her to strike my father on the arm with it. The night of the performance, when she hit him, he forgot his lines. Earlier in the day, he had been given a vaccine in just the spot where the rolling pin would land. That sudden, glinting pain on stage made him, for a moment, lose whatever he was supposed to say. And, after the performance, he spoke furiously to my mother, cursing her clumsiness.

"Why the hell did you hit me so hard?"

∾

Three days after my arrival in Vienna, I came down with the flu. My bedroom was an oven of sleeping, the blankets pushed off, a sudden heat and perspiration staining the pajamas that stuck to my skin. In the middle of the night, I wandered to the bathroom down the hall to drink some water from the faucet. In the mirror, my face was fever-blurred, unfamiliar as a stranger's. And then a spinning. Down, down. When I came to, I could feel that I was on the floor. I lay under the sink, the porcelain basin and metal pipes above me. I stayed like this for an hour, the tiles so chilled they hurt, and the hurt felt almost good against my skin.

∾

That winter, exhausted and sick, I didn't visit any of the usual Viennese landmarks. Not St. Stephen's Cathedral with its tolling bells and gothic glittering of spires. Not the Rathausplatz, although it was Christmastime and the square was crowded with vendors' stalls: merchants selling hand-carved wooden horses, blown-glass beads on leather cords, decorations made of gingerbread, and of course mugs of spiced red wine hot enough to warm the hands. And not the Österreichische Galerie Belvedere, the museum where Gustav Klimt's famed portraits of Adele Bloch-Bauer had been on display since 1941, following their seizure by the Nazis during the Anschluss.

I didn't stand before the painting that the Austrians had renamed *The Woman in Gold*. They called the portrait by this title to conceal its prove-nance and subject, that it depicted the face—pale skin and a swirl of black hair—of one of Vienna's most celebrated Jewish women, Adele Bloch-Bauer: socialite, patron of the arts, and hostess of a salon that was renowned for its sparkling conversations with some of the greatest musicians, artists, and intellectuals of the day.

Klimt first painted Adele Bloch-Bauer in 1901, her features recognizable in his depiction of Judith holding the decapitated head of Holofernes, her body draped in sheer fabrics, her breasts bare. By 1907, he had completed work on the first of two commissioned portraits of Adele. He placed her figure in an expanse of gold and silver leaf, adorning her with markings that scholars have deemed erotic. In Anne Marie O'Connor's international bestseller *The Lady in Gold*, the author writes that "[t]he painting seemed alive with meaning. The Egyptian eyes of Horus floated on a tapestry with stylized vulvular symbols . . . Klimt embedded Adele in a luminous field of real gold leaf, giving her the appearance of a religious icon, which art his-torians would compare to the mosaic portrait of Empress Theodora in Ravenna."

A second commissioned portrait of Adele followed five years later, this one more muted, less sensual, more a study of how a body might be posi-tioned within misty rectangles of red, pink, green, and lilac. As O'Connor recounts in her book, the ownership of these two paintings became the subject of several international lawsuits, with Bloch-Bauer's niece, Maria Altmann, fighting for the repatriation of her family's stolen art. When Alt-mann eventually won the judgment, the paintings were brought to the

United States in 2006, where they were sold with the stipulation that the buyers make the works available for public display. Today, *The Woman in Gold*—now known again as *Portrait of Adele Bloch-Bauer I*—is on display at the Neue Gallerie in New York.

Often, when people discuss the case of the seized Klimt paintings, they wonder what Adele would have wished if she had lived to see the Nazi invasion and the Austrian collaboration that followed. As the US Holocaust Memorial Museum explains, when the German troops entered the country on March 12, 1935, "[t]hey received the enthusiastic support of most of the population." Adele Bloch-Bauer died in 1925 of meningitis. She left a will asking that her portraits be displayed in the Galerie Belvedere. Thirteen years later, her husband was forced to run from Vienna, leaving behind many of his possessions. After the war, other members of the family attempted to reclaim these valuables but failed, for decades, in their efforts. If Adele had lived to witness Germany's annexation of Austria and the Austrian collaboration that followed, would she have continued to view herself as both Jewish and Viennese? Would she have believed the regal city by the Danube was her home?

℘

Sacher Torte, too, was once the subject of a lawsuit, fought between the Hotel Sacher and the Demel Café. It took nine years for the case to be settled out of court, with the Hotel Sacher winning the right to call itself the purveyor of the "original" version of the cake.

℘

Rabbi and chocolate expert Deborah R. Prinz writes about the birth of this beloved confection in *The Forward*: "At just 16 years old, a Jewish cook's apprentice named Franz Sacher revolutionized the pastry world with an impromptu creation that came to be known as the Sacher Torte." Prinz explains that "[i]n 1832 Sacher was working in the kitchen of Prince Klemens Wenzel von Metternich (1773-1859), the chancellor of Vienna, when the head chef fell ill. Everyone turned to the young Sacher, expecting him to create a new dessert for the special guests that evening. He came up with a dense, dark chocolate cake with apricot jam filling, which pleased the crowd—and has continued to be a crowd-pleaser ever since."

But Sacher Torte is more than a crowd-pleaser. It's a story about being a Jew. A young Jewish baker created a cake that became the very essence of Vienna. If a city could be said to have a flavor, Vienna's would be chocolate paired with apricot jam. It would be the dry crumb of the cake and the glistening fruit preserve, the one flavor placed surprisingly alongside the other.

When it comes to Franz Sacher, I don't want to speak of assimilation. Historically, for Jews, the word has meant a loss of language, a loss of religion, a disappearance, even a betrayal. I would rather speak about the painful desire to belong. In Sacher's era and in the next century, there were many Jews who defined Vienna, what the city thought and listened to, how the city dressed. They must have believed that belonging would be possible, if they spoke the language of the place, if they learned the rhythm of its streets, if they made themselves useful or necessary. If. If. If.

"Between 1860 and 1900," writes O'Connor, "the Jewish population of Vienna exploded, from 6,000 to 147,000, the largest in West Europe . . . Affluent Jewish families were instant lovers of Viennese culture. They filled the empire's new theaters, opera houses, and schools far out of proportion to their share of the population." Sigmund Freud—who is said to have loved Sacher Torte—diagnosed the corseted women of the Ringstrasse. Gustav Mahler converted to Catholicism; under his directorship, the Vienna Court Opera gave performances of works by Wagner, including *Das Rheingold*, *Siegfried*, *Tannhäuser*, and *Die Walküre*. And Adele Bloch-Bauer posed for a painting, one hand bent down at a right angle and the other hand covering the first, her fingers intimate and sharp, as if the two halves of her body didn't know one another, as if she were a golden stranger even to herself.

☙

One time at a concert in Vienna, my father rose from his chair, leaning against the wall behind him. It wasn't crowded that night, and his body felt too stiff to sit. An usher, official and rigid in his uniform, approached him.

"Go back to your seat," he told my father.

"Now I know why the Austrians were such good Nazis," my father hissed back.

But tonight at dinner, as I talk about this essay, my father grimaces, "I have good memories of Vienna too." He recalls the local grocer who presented my father with a great bouquet of cellophaned flowers as a gift for my mother. "Your writing is usually more nuanced than to simply say a place was bad," my father reproaches.

When he asks this of me—this kind of generosity toward the Austrians—should I interpret his request as wanting to belong, wanting to find warmth on windy boulevards? Maybe. So, in deference to my father, I'll place the grocer's thoughtful blossoms on a table next to other objects from our time in Vienna, amber glasses of beer and plates of flaky strudel, the pale filling spilling from the folds of pastry.

***

I was sick for most of the winter break, only leaving the apartment a few times. I stayed indoors, wishing the rooms would stop swirling with vertigo, my vision a dizzy whoosh of snow. In the afternoons, I worked my way through *Daniel Deronda*. I had fallen in love with George Eliot's prose the previous school year when we studied *Middlemarch* in our junior seminar. "I will always be a Jewess," says Mirah Lapidoth about halfway through *Daniel Deronda*. "I will love Christians when they are good, like you. But I will always cling to my people. I will always worship with them." I knew Eliot's novel had been critiqued for her treatment of Jewish characters—the concern that Mirah and even Daniel Deronda himself lacked complexity—but, reading these lines, I thought about what it meant for a Jew like me to be in a city like Vienna. I was not one who worshipped. But did I cling to my people? Would I always be a Jewess?

Recently, I was on the phone with a friend who is the daughter of two Holocaust survivors. For the past three years, we have talked into the late hours about where, if anywhere, we belong. We are insomniacs together. When it seems the rest of the world is already curled beneath the woolen weight of sleep, she texts me. Or I text her. *Are you still up.* On the phone the other night, I could hear the worry in her speech. She is in the process of applying for teaching positions at lush, green campuses around the country, places where the buildings are engraved with the names of donors long dead. She has revised her cover letter hundreds of times.

"Is it too Jewish?" she asked.

"We're always too Jewish," I said. "For the people who hate Jews, we will always be too Jewish."

"You're right," she said, "of course you're right."

As I listened to her voice on the other end of the line, I pulled on one of the black ringlets hanging down into my face. The frizzy spiral of hair lengthened, then sprang back into its previous, tightly coiled form when I let it go. I slid a finger down the length of my nose. I felt the angle of my cheekbone. If someone were to paint a portrait of me, would the canvas be renamed, its Jewish provenance erased? Would I someday float, anonymous and unspeaking, in a gleaming plane of gold?

ॐ

I don't remember the end of my time in Vienna. Five and a half years before, when our family left our diplomatic posting in Poland, I tried not to cry as we drove away from our home for the last time, our car pulling out of the long driveway. If I close my eyes now, I can still see the house in Warsaw set down squarely among overgrown bushes and evergreens. I can re-create each room, the foyer leading into a wide hall with doorways to the kitchen and living room, one flight of stairs going down to the basement and another turning a corner to the second floor. My memory can wander upward. I can walk into my brother's room where, as a toddler, he once grabbed a large plastic container of baby powder, squeezing it between his small, sturdy hands, so that every object in the space was suddenly a dusty shadow, powder on every surface, my brother's great blue eyes blinking and uncanny in the whitened air. "Our little Aryan," we used to call him.

I can visit my mother's bathroom where I got my first period, sit again on the toilet facing the tub, touch the cramping wetness between my legs. I can climb more stairs to my bedroom at the top of the house. Here is the closet where I used to stand among my clothes, considering which dress or shirt might make me disappear. Here is the bright bathroom where I first learned to shave my legs. My classmates had left a letter in my locker. My body hair was *disgusting*, they wrote. *You disgust us.* The day after I read those words, I sat on the bathtub, spreading a thick layer of foam across my legs, the brown fuzz hidden beneath a snowy field of shaving cream. I cried as the blade nicked my knees and the tender creases at my ankles. But it felt good, too, to inflict these small red lines of hurt.

Although I loved Poland, the country was frequently unkind to me. The Jewish girl who barely understood her Jewishness was spat at on the playground, told to burn, go up in smoke. I was asked once if it was true that I *drank the blood of babies*. Before gym class, in the changing room, a girl reached over to touch the top of my head.

"Where are your horns?" she said.

I was sitting on a bench tugging on my sneaker when her fingertips pushed against my scalp, as if she were feeling around for something lost in the dark. I bent toward my laces, fumbling to tie a bow. My eyes glossed over with tears.

Austria never wounded me in this way. It was polite and chilly; it had good table manners. And I never learned to love it. Perhaps this explains why I don't remember leaving.

ↇ

The obedience of the Viennese. Their patience, waiting at the box office to buy tickets in the cold. The velvet seats of concert halls. The dimming lights. The programs shut, the unwhispering. The deep quiet of listening. And then the audience standing, as if in unison, to applaud.

ↇ

All these decades later, I ask myself: Why love what might not love us back? Why try to belong to a place that might eventually push us out? Why speak languages that might be used to call us disloyal? Sometimes I am dizzy with questions, almost fevered with them.

On the news, there have been men marching with raised torches. They shout, "Jews will not replace us." At a synagogue, in a neighborhood where I once spent a summer, there is a massacre, the shooter enraged that organizations like the Hebrew Immigrant Aid Society should offer help to refugees. Five people are stabbed at a Chanukah party, six gunned down in a kosher market. On the internet, if I click on the wrong links, I see cartoon drawings of hooked noses or gleeful photographs of a crematorium oven, the door left open, gray piles of ash inside.

Now, when my father bakes a Sacher Torte, I ask for extra jam between the layers, although this is not the traditional way to prepare the dessert. My grandmother's recipe calls for the apricot preserves to be spread "very thinly." But aren't we, I tell myself—even after all the failures to belong, in the marble cities of Europe or even here in the United States, in neighborhoods with names like Summer Oaks, where people nod and smile, *hello good morning how are you*—aren't we still hungry for the syrupy reduction of stone fruit, globs and globs of it? Aren't we hungrier than ever for the cake? Don't we still crave the way the apricot jam sweetens, is made sweeter, when placed alongside the chocolate, its abiding bitterness?

The Resonator

Every day for four months, I laid my bag of research materials in a plastic tray and watched it slide through the steady gaze of the X-ray machine. I stepped through the narrow arch of the metal detector. I smiled at the guards. And then—having crossed from the present into a structure built to commemorate the past, all the stone and metal and brick engraved with history—I walked into the United States Holocaust Memorial Museum, the USHMM. Usually I was there before the crowds arrived. I turned a few corners, until I reached the hidden, private elevators that would take me up, up to the wing of the building where the other scholars hunched at their desks.

I was at the Museum on an academic fellowship to write poems about trauma: how it is held in the many rooms of the body, how it is a raw edge, how it is a cracked handful of refracting glass. These poems, I hoped, would become part of my dissertation, a collection of creative writing that considered my own relationship to genocide, a family inheritance. Sitting in my cubicle, I took notes from books with titles like *Generations of the Holocaust* and *The Legacy of the Holocaust*. Each new poem was a process of rapid thought followed by long pauses. I often stood, moved away from the computer screen to wander the Museum, then returned minutes or hours later to study the way light fell across my words.

Around me were the sounds of other fingers tapping on keyboards, PhD candidates in history or philosophy or psychology, all of them typing long chapters of their dissertations, and the stacks of books beside them even taller than my own.

At the Museum, I began to work on a new manuscript written in the invented voice of a woman named Ida Lewin. I imagined Ida living and dying between the wars in a nonexistent Polish town, Zawsze-Zima, or Always-Winter. Whatever Ida saw of the Shoah came as visions, nightmares from which she woke soaked with sweat. Ida wrote poems of her own, little scraps of Yiddish that were dug up from the ground decades later, each text eaten through with holes:

> There is a trembling in me, half
> like when I bend down to pray
> and half like the late night
> of longing . . .

I coughed or cleared my throat and could feel Ida's speech like a rough cube of sugar dissolving on my tongue.

ↄↄ

It was strange to be a poet in that place. When I introduced myself to the other research fellows, I wondered if my presence worried some.

"I'm a poet. I'm writing about intergenerational trauma," I would say, attempting to sound confident about my project.

"A poet?" one young historian laughed. "I didn't know those were allowed here."

Allowed. During the rest of my time at the Museum, I thought a lot about what this meant.

In my head, I conducted a series of conversations with the young historian: "Are my poems inappropriate?" I asked her. "Am I?" I imagined showing her my drafts, pointing to the ways in which verse, too, might engage with research just as her own writing did. I could see us standing among the library stacks, facing one another, our backs pressed against the metal shelves, our whispers like a fierce shuffling of notecards.

But I was too nervous to talk with her. I never approached the desk where she sat marking the pages of thick books with tiny flags of paper.

In my fellowship application, I had anticipated concerns about my work. "I know historians often worry that Holocaust literature risks 'getting the facts wrong,'" I wrote, "sometimes sacrificing historical accuracy for the sake of literary affect." I had argued that I would use the Museum's resources to write poems that maintained "both literary and scholarly integrity." But even with these reassurances, I wasn't sure I could persuade a historian or a social scientist that poems belonged here. Elie Wiesel, perhaps the most famous Holocaust survivor in the world, had frequently critiqued art's ability to engage with the Shoah:

> Auschwitz represents the negation and failure of human progress; it negates the human design and casts doubts on its validity. Then, it defeated culture; later, it defeated art, because just as no one could imagine Auschwitz before Auschwitz, no one can now retell Auschwitz after Auschwitz. The truth of Auschwitz remains hidden in its ashes. Only those who lived it in their flesh and in their minds can possibly transform their experience into knowledge. Others, despite their best intentions, can never do so.

I understood Wiesel's anxieties. Those who lived genocide "in their flesh" would make art that functioned as testimony: *I saw this, I heard this, I was there*. Those who came later—the children and grandchildren of survivors—would interact with the Shoah as history. They would puncture the pieties of trauma, question whether pain does anything but shatter us. They would experiment with narrative, twist time and point of view as a way of demonstrating how atrocity challenges linear storytelling. Straight lines, the direct movement from point A to point B, no longer make sense in a world after Auschwitz.

But did it follow that because "no one could imagine Auschwitz before Auschwitz," therefore "no one can retell Auschwitz after Auschwitz"? Imagination and retrospection were not the same. And the Shoah needed to be recounted in many ways, I kept telling myself, first through the testimony of survivors and later as a narrative based in the research of scholars across disciplines, history and law and medicine and sociology, but also in the stories that artists create. The crime was interdisciplinary; the effort to confront it could be, too.

To reach the room that held the research fellows, I had to cross a floating walkway embedded with glass bricks, the floor illuminated by the air beneath. While my work differed from the scholars', we all moved through the same architecture, feeling how the building shaped our thinking, contained us with its heavy materials. We were all participating in acts of interpretation. Theirs were accompanied by footnotes and citations and mine were marked by stanza breaks.

ভা

Soon, Ida's voice grew louder. "Go on with my poems," she told me:

There is a trembling in me, half
like bending to pray
and half like the late night
of longing
          My ears are filled
with the feather-soft of air.
On such occasions
                    Who can blame me
for feeling afraid . . .

When I sat at the computer, I could hear Ida talking. After a few days, Ida began to whisper in other parts of the Museum, the corridors that led from one display to the next, the stairs with their dark ascents.

ভা

When I wasn't writing, I spent much of my days studying different parts of the Museum. Sometimes I left my desk to avoid the work I had assigned myself. Sometimes a change of perspective knocked a poem loose from its stuck place. Many afternoons, I sat on a stone bench in the nearby Hall of Remembrance and watched visitors light the memorial candles, how the eternal flame twitched and ghosted before a black wall inscribed with a quote from Deuteronomy. Or I stood on the first floor in the Hall of Witnesses, an echoing entryway of raw brick and distant skylights, the ceiling spanned by steel trusses. The USHMM's website explains that the purpose of this area is to "'impound' the visitor and send disturbing signals of separation." It comforted me to read the Museum's description of itself, metaphor used to describe the building's intended effect.

Most of all, I liked walking the building's staircases and bridges, the halls that led to conference rooms and temporary exhibits. Their in-betweenness reminded me of poetry, because the best poems don't ask a reader to respond in only one way. They are open, leading us in many directions.

Frequently, I went to those liminal spaces to stare at the Museum's four site-specific art installations on display. First, there was Sol LeWitt's wall drawing *Consequence*, a series of five textured squares, large enough to fill a long wall, bordered by black and trembling with quiet fields of color. Located in a lounge on the second floor of the permanent exhibition, the piece asks viewers to consider all the definitions of "consequence." What can be inferred. What is caused. What is important.

Near the outdoor plaza, where I ate my bagged lunch every day, stood Joel Shapiro's *Loss and Regeneration*. The bronze sculpture contains two parts: a tall, branching figure, cantilevered and precarious, and a smaller wedge that tilts into the brick ground below. Like so much of Shapiro's work, the piece feels as if it is about to shift, despite the mass of its materials. Staring at *Loss and Regeneration*, I often felt as if I were seesawing between belief and doubt. My poems were part of the necessary work of chronicling genocide. No, they were trivial and bad.

And then there was Richard Serra's *Gravity*, a huge square of steel wedged in the stairs at one of the corners of the Hall of Witnesses. The metal seemed to chew the floor, consume the ground. "*Gravity* activates space," writes art historian James Romaine, "and by extension activates our movement. Serra's work gives form to our sense of descending into the history of the Holocaust as memorialized throughout the exhibits on that floor." I could see what he meant. Sometimes I took the steps to the left of Serra's piece and sometimes to the right, always feeling how the art changed the shape of my passage, creating a steel barrier along one of my sides or the other. If the positioning of a sculpture could so easily affect my own movements, then how might walls and roadblocks and electrified fences have altered the paths of those who tried to run from National Socialism?

Of all four installations, Ellsworth Kelly's *Memorial* was the one I visited most often. Positioned on the third floor, *Memorial* is an immense sculpture in four parts, massive planes of white projecting from the walls to create depth and shadow. According to the Museum's website, Kelly compared them "to memorial tablets that, in their anonymity, bear the names of all the victims of the Holocaust." The panels reminded me of the blank page waiting. When I felt wedged in my own words, not knowing what to write next, I would visit *Memorial* and ask myself: What should be said? Can I say it?

Consequence, *Loss and Remembrance*, *Gravity*, and *Memorial* were each created in collaboration with James Ingo Freed, the architect who designed the USHMM. They are the only pieces of contemporary art displayed in the Museum. They reject literal representations of horror in favor of abstraction, large plains of canvas or metal onto which viewers can project their questions, their anger, their grief. Should art, should artists have a place in a memorial to the Shoah? These installations suggested that the answer was *yes*. But I came to recognize that the building itself gives an additional response, that the Museum is also a thing of artifice and artfulness. It, too, is art.

In an interview, Freed explains that the purpose of the Museum is to "act as a resonator for the memories of others." The structure, he argues, "is not meant to be an architectural walk, or a walk through memory, or an exposition of emotion, but all of this. I want to leave it open as a resonator of emotions. Odd or quiet is not enough. It must be intestinal, visceral; it must take you in its grip." No matter how frequently I stood in the public elevators that took visitors to the permanent exhibition on the third floor, my body pressed tightly against the many bodies of tourists, I could feel how all of us resonated with nervousness at what we would see when the gleaming doors swished open. We vibrated before the glass case displaying thousands of shoes from Auschwitz. We shivered within the Tower of Faces, a room three stories tall, its walls filled with black and white photographic reproductions, documentary evidence of the hundreds of families from a murdered town in Lithuania, the images hung nearly to the top of the vaulted ceiling.

It wasn't simply that each display was skillfully organized. As scholar Edward T. Linenthal explains in *Preserving Memory: The Struggle to Create America's Holocaust Museum*, the USHMM "would have to communicate through raw materials and organization of the space the feel of inexorable, forced movement: disruption, alienation, constriction, observation, selection." Freed argues that his architecture provides "an evocation of the incomplete. Irresolution, imbalances are built in." Nonetheless, despite its many ambiguities, the Museum is designed in such a way that visitors are compelled to follow a guided route; they cannot choose which gates to enter or what bridges to cross or when they might encounter high walls, the Museum having determined the path tourists take through history.

In the Tower of Faces, where a tourist looks into the eyes of the murdered, a thousand photographs staring back, the doorways arch in the manner of old European structures: for instance, the entries to train stations or synagogues. And yet, the Museum is not a simulacrum. Its architecture does not replicate the exact sensations of visiting the Gare du Nord in Paris or the shuls on Szeroka Street in Kraków. Rather, the metal rivets, exposed brick, and hewn stone, as the Museum's website points out, remind viewers of "construction methods from the industrial past" and offer "an ironic criticism of early modernism's lofty ideals of reason and order that were perverted to build the factories of death."

Drifting through the Museum, I often thought about the building's power to pull visitors into trauma or else release us from it. Light made every difference. Depending on the time of day or the weather, the walls could devour me with grief, or the openings to the outside could cast a sudden light across my footsteps.

Literary scholar Jeffrey Jerome Cohen writes that the USHMM "enacts this emotional capture through ample use of stone, the proper material in which to encapsulate weighty memory. Stone and glass are the most common materials for constructing Holocaust memorials: ponderous and earthbound remembrance combine with a sky-directed futurity, a hopefulness." At the Museum, the light came from below as well as from the windows overhead. Each morning, I walked across the glass bridge that led to my cubicle. Sometimes the floor glowed, and I was held up by it. Sometimes, on rainy days, the floor felt like an absence, the surface gone dark, and I was falling through my poems.

☙

Ida kept telling me, "Revise, revise":

> Like a leaf on a branch,
> I tremble at
>   the weather,
>   creased along the blade,
> my margin torn as if by the teeth
> of an animal. A late storm approaches.
>
> I turn
>   with the quill-sharp air.
> On such occasions
>   Who can blame me
> for fearing,
>   even my stem might snap.
>
> There is something coming,
>   the bark of the tree
> is marked as though with ink
>   —some scrawled prophecy.

Ida knew she belonged in the Museum. She spoke because sometimes beauty travels anywhere it wants.

℘

Near the end of my fellowship, I gave a public presentation about my project. I stood at the front of a large conference room, my damp hand squeezing the remote control I would use to advance the slides projected behind me.

"A poet? I didn't know those were allowed here," the young historian had said to me months before. I thought of her laughter as I clicked through each slide, the light touching the edge of my arm. Here were five strategies, I said, gesturing at the screen, that I employed when trying to write a good—no, not just a good but an ethical—poem about the Shoah.

I read from the numbered points: *one*, that the poem must explore the relationship between form and content, *two*, that the poem must show knowledge of so-called canonical Holocaust texts and of genocide studies, *three*, that the poem must manipulate or reinterpret tropes of the field, *four*, that the poem must engage in intertextuality, hybridity, or interdisciplinarity, and *five*, that the poem must engage in self-reflective thinking.

And then I recited some of Ida Lewin's fragments. I could picture her seated in one of the plastic chairs at the edge of the room. She listened to my translations of her words from the original Yiddish, although, of course, there was no original Yiddish, only what I imagined she might have written in a language I didn't know. Out of my research of the interwar period in Poland and of Jewish writers in those years, I had invented her brown hair and the line of buttons down the front of her gray dress. I could see her small feet laced tightly into a pair of leather boots.

When I finished speaking, one of the other fellows, a scholar from Germany, smiled at me.

"You mean every day you were writing these poems?"

Throughout the four months of my fellowship, I was always leaving my desk to wander the Museum. I would return hours later with a few new notes in my tiny black notebook. I might have slouched in my chair then, stared at the flickering cursor on my computer screen, typing nothing, not even mouthing the shard of language before me.

I must have looked like I wasn't doing any work at all.

∾

After four months at the Museum, I decided that the poems arrived like ominous trains pulling into a station. If the building functioned as a resonator, then positioned within the structure for those four months, I began to resonate in my own small way as well.

Once I left the Museum, I stopped hearing Ida's voice. That building, I decided, held hollow spaces designed to magnify echoes, waves of speech. The walls reflected each sound.

∾

A few days after my presentation, I logged out of my computer. I returned my borrowed books to the research librarian. I was done. Ida's poems eventually became a book. Years after the fellowship, when I flipped through the pages of the collection and read what I had written, I didn't see myself. I saw a visitation, as if Ida had been a revenant speaking through me. I had researched the extinguished Jewish towns of Eastern Europe, studied Yiddish culture of the early twentieth century, and in return Ida gave me her voice for a little while.

Beyond the young historian, no one else confronted me during my residency at the Museum. Nobody shook a finger in my face or shouted *You don't belong here!* I often thought of the USHMM as filled with unexpected joy, people searching databases or hunched over an artifact from the archives, doing the meaningful work of testimony and witness in a building positioned, symbolically, near the National Mall, what Edward T. Linenthal calls "the ceremonial center of the nation." Still, I constantly asked myself: Was I atrocious for writing poems in a place that commemorates atrocity? Or was I simply making the beautiful in a building I saw as beautiful?

When contemplating the Shoah, it is natural to think of the world as entirely dark. "We shovel a grave in the air," writes Paul Celan. And in another poem, he says, "They dug and heard nothing more." In sites across Europe, the sky once filled with ash. The ground crowded with shadows.

But at the Museum, when I crossed the overpass of glass bricks, I saw that sometimes, unexpectedly, the light can come from below, because that's where the dead reside. That's where they call from. That's where their knowledge dwells.

You Must Stumble

The memorials are made of concrete and covered in brass. Each one is the size and shape of a small cobblestone, measuring 96 by 96 millimeters. They're called Stolpersteine in German. Stumbling stones.

Gunter Demnig first conceived of the Stolpersteine in the early 1990s. As Kirsten Grieshaber recounts in the *New York Times*, the idea began when Demnig painted a "white line through the city, showing where decades earlier" members of the Romani population "had been chased through the streets to the train station." Confronted by an elderly woman who told him that Roma had never lived in Cologne—*never*, the woman insisted, *never*—Demnig began to think about how the erased past might be made visible and palpable in the present.

Within the next two years, he began embedding small commemorations in the earth. Each stone represents one person, the words "here lived" etched across the metal. Demnig positions the stone in front of the last place the person chose to live. "It goes beyond our comprehension to understand the killing of six million Jews," the artist explains, "But if you read the name of one person, calculate his age, look at his old home and wonder behind which window he used to live, then the horror has a face to it."

I first learned of Demnig's project several years ago, while I was working on a book of poems. I wrote that history was "a rock protruding." Once I finished the poem, I forgot about the Stolpersteine.

Or perhaps it's more accurate to say I filed away this form of memorialization in the huge catalogue of the Shoah that is stored inside of me. I have spent the last twenty years studying this field. Academic coursework. Summer and winter programs in the interdisciplinarity of the Holocaust, how history and literature and art and theory must overlap to tell the full story of the horror. I lived for two months in the town of Oświęcim, or Auschwitz as it's more commonly known. I have read hundreds of books on the subject, seen hundreds of films.

In other words, I am able not to weep when I read Anthony Hecht's poem "The Book of Yolek" to a roomful of students: "the electric fences, the numeral tattoo." At a screening of *Night and Fog*, I barely gulp with nausea when the bulldozers—with their huge, mechanical claws—shovel the knotted shapes that used to be people. If I give a presentation about the work of poets attempting to represent atrocity on the page, my focus is research and rigor; it is ethos and logos rather than pathos. "People often rely too heavily," I warn the audience, "on the horror of the narrative to do the intellectual and emotional work of the text."

In the Stolpersteine project, every stone is grounded in research, the rigor of getting the names and dates right. The brass shines yellow-orange but is no less powerful for the coldness of its gleaming. In fact, if a pedestrian were to kneel before a stumbling stone, she might discover her own face reflected in its smooth surface.

℘

I keep tripping over the crack between presence and absence. On Yom Kippur, I receive an email from a third cousin in London: a woman whose name I have never heard before. She is writing, my third cousin says, to repair the damage of a feud—a "broigus," she calls it—that occurred between her mother and my paternal grandmother fifty years ago. After all, she says, it is the High Holy Days. In this season, we atone. We throw scraps of paper in the water and watch them float away. We acknowledge the dead.

When I tell my father about the email, he shakes his head. "I have no memory of any of this," he says—not the fight from five decades ago, not the woman who was once so close to his own mother (both of them named Johanna for the same ancestor), none of it. How is this possible? I wonder. How can a quarrel have so hurt these distant relatives, while on our side of the family, the conflict became not so much silence but nothing, a hollow where a story could reside?

Along with the email, my third cousin sends me a series of charts indicating how we are linked. In one of the boxes on the chart, I locate my great-grandfather, Markus Meyer, born August 12, 1876, in Mülheim, a city in the western corner of Germany. According to the chart, Markus died on May 2, 1942, in Łódź.

Łódź. 1942. I know the story of this place.

৵

I write to my third cousin, asking about my great-grandfather. I want to know: "Did Markus die as a result of the horrible conditions in the ghetto? Or was he part of one of the liquidations to Chełmno?"

But nothing. She doesn't respond. After fifty years of silence between the two sides of the family—a quiet I couldn't hear until now—there is more unspeaking between us.

And because my third cousin has never written to me again, I am left to stare at the charts she sent me. I try to make a narrative of the names. I tell myself I will gather breadcrumbs in a forest where the birdsong sounds like shrieking. I will find a way to the candied house, to the cage or the oven.

I type in my internet search engine: *Łódź ghetto 1942.* "In January 1942," *The Holocaust Encyclopedia* informs me, "German authorities began to deport Jews from Lodz to the Chelmno killing center. By September 1942, they had deported over 70,000 Jews and about 5,000 Roma to Chelmno." I click on a hyperlink. I read that Chełmno "was the first stationary facility where poison gas was used for mass murder of Jews." Of course, I know from my studies that, in Jewish folklore, Chełm was also the great shtetl of fools, a town of tilting houses and tangled streets. The tales of Chełm show every problem is solved by making a different problem. A hole is dug in the ground to fill another hole. A man is selected to do the worrying for all the people in the village; his payment will be a ruble. But what, then, the others wonder—with that kind of money in his pocket—will he have to worry about?

I think of a story I used to teach in a class on American Jewish writers. Nathan Englander's "The Tumblers" shows the intersection of the Chełm of literary tradition with the real Chełmno of genocide. In "The Tumblers," a group of devout Jews disguise themselves as a troupe of circus performers to escape deportation. Costumed in scraps of upholstery fabric, they cartwheel and crabwalk for a crowd of Nazis. The story ends not with murder but with the schlemiels still trapped in their tattered disguises, leaping forever in the "harsh and unforgiving" spotlight of history. They remain held between circles of glaring light and the dark beyond.

თ

As writer Andreas Kluth explains, "Demnig calls his project 'a decentralised monument' or, alternatively, 'a social sculpture.'" The earliest Stolpersteine were placed illegally in Berlin. "Three months later," says Kluth, "the plates—51 of them, all along one street—came to the attention of the authorities when the stones impeded construction work. They wanted to remove them, but the workers refused. Bureaucrats came to inspect the stones, and they were retrospectively legalized."

Now there are more than seventy-five thousand stumbling stones embedded in the streets and sidewalks of twenty-four European countries. All Stolpersteine are "made by hand," Demnig's website states, "in direct opposition to the Nazis' mass extermination policies," the concrete blocks individually molded, the brass stamped with their painful specifics. There are hard stories beneath the feet of pedestrians. Sometimes the metal catches the light and someone kneels to read a name, a date. *Here lived*, says the ground.

This endeavor of making the forgotten visible recalls the work of American Jewish artist Shimon Attie. From 1991 to 1996, Attie created a series of installations using photographic projections. In Berlin, for instance, he cast black and white images of exterminated Jewish life against the brick walls and old doors of the city. Then he photographed what he saw, his pictures illuminating the break between what exists now and what once was: an Orthodox man standing before a table, a woman leaning out of a window, a stranger staring at the display in a Yiddish bookstore.

James Young, the noted Holocaust scholar, writes of Attie:

> He knows that this presence of the past is apparent only to those
> already familiar with a site's history or to those who actually carry
> a visual memory of this site from another, earlier time . . . Without
> historical consciousness of visitors, these sites remain essentially indif-
> ferent to their pasts, altogether amnesiac. They "know" only what we
> know, "remember" only what we remember.

So too with the stumbling stones. Without the gleaming surfaces of memory—brass inscribed with a name, a date—these ordinary sites in Cologne
and Prague and Salzburg would continue to know nothing, remember
nothing. Without the stumbling stones, we would not be able to point to
nearby buildings and say, "Here lived and here and here."

✍

For a few days, I haven't been able to leave *The Holocaust Encyclopedia*. I
click on the link for "gas." Under the heading for "Chelmno," I learn that
"[i]n 1941, the SS concluded that the deportation of Jews to killing centers
(to be gassed) was the most efficient way of achieving the 'Final Solution.'"
I could go on like this, clicking forever, traveling the gray path of hyperlinks from gas to Final Solution to Kristallnacht to pogroms. In the circu-
lar way of fairytales, I might end up back again at Łódź, still trying to learn
what happened to Markus.

The next week, I wander through the online database of Yad Vashem,
the World Holocaust Remembrance Center in Jerusalem. Last / Maiden
Name: Meyer. First Name: Markus. Place: Lodz. And here he is: Markus
Meyer, born 1876 "to Isaak and Sara. He was married to Theresia nee Baer.
Prior to WWII he lived in Koeln, Germany." And here he is again: "During
the war he was in Litzmannstadt, Poland. Markus was murdered in the
Shoah."

"Murdered in the Shoah" should be an answer to how Markus died. It isn't. The phrase can mean death camps and gas, as well as mass shootings in an anonymous forest or field. It can mean the random killings that occurred during roundups and inspections. It can mean famine or sickness. It can mean so many different brutalities that it means almost nothing but entirely, entirely gone.

Furthermore, Litzmannstadt is not a place I recognize. I return to my search engine, type the letters in the box. And now I'm back yet again at Łódź, because the Germans renamed the city Litzmannstadt. Names were always changing in that time, streets and even people. Even ordinary words—"oven," for instance, and "chimney"—were transformed. They now held their own kind of terrible heat.

All of this reminds me of Judy Budnitz's short story "Hershel," another text I know well from my teaching of contemporary American Jewish literature. In a tiny village in the "old country," children were once born with the help of the shtetl's "baby maker." He made each baby out of dough, kneading the form until it was the right consistency, then placing it in a bowl to rise. Once the dough was ready, Hershel molded it into the shape of an infant. "Then," the narrator goes on, "he would slide the baby on its back into the oven . . . The babies shifted and bubbled as they baked, rocking on their backs." The babies baked like this for nine months, until they were ready. "Nothing could compare to the sight of a new baby fresh from the oven, crisp at the fingernails, crying from the cold as Hershel held him aloft, checking for any mistakes in his handiwork."

Reading "Hershel," it's impossible not to think of the other ovens, with their arched doors and their great capacity for burning. Although Budnitz's story attempts to transform the oven back into a symbol of nourishment—a place where babies are born—the story ends by acknowledging how history can devour metaphor. The baby maker is just as entirely gone as my great-grandfather, so many of the fictional characters and real people who dwell within me, destroyed by the same genocide.

cs

For the next few weeks, I type "Markus Meyer" and "Łódź" and "1942" in the search engine, clicking on links deeper and deeper in the pages of results. All this information is indeed a forest. "Midway in the journey of life," Dante writes, "I came to myself in a dark wood, / for the straight way was lost." In looking for what happened to Markus Meyer, am I coming to myself at the midway of my life?

I have become a fool of Chełm, digging one hole to fill another. Each time I search for Markus, I forget why I'm looking. I am lost in my own familiar ritual of research, losing sight of the man who was my great-grandfather. He is buried beneath facts and statistics about the millions of dead.

Or I have become a woman forever tumbling through the past. Look how I dance and crabwalk from one horror to another.

Or I am Hershel the baby maker, and I can't decide if the oven is a box that bakes new life or burns it.

There is a choice to make in the dark wood. This pursuit of Markus's death offers an answer about who I am. Or else it tells me nothing about myself and, in constantly returning to the Shoah, I have become unable to live in the right now. Flipping through the TV channels, I inevitably come upon a movie about a photographer in Mauthausen or a police procedural drama in which the plotline focuses on rare coins once stolen from a Holocaust survivor. I find genocide everywhere, as if my compass always points me toward mass graves and executions.

But just as I'm beginning to question whether I should continue looking, I click on the images the search engine has found. And here is Markus once more. The first picture in the top row is a photograph of his name stamped on a Stolperstein. It's a close-up of a grouping of four stumbling stones, a pair of couples, Markus and Theresia Meyer placed above Ernst and Irma Schönholz, their four names forming a square configuration of the murdered. My great-grandfather's Stolperstein reads:

Hier Wohnte
Markus Meyer
Jg. 1876
Deportiert 1941

Łódź
Für Tot Erklärt

In English, this means:

Here Lived
Markus Meyer
Born 1876
Deported 1941
Łódź
Declared Dead

In the photograph, tender stubs of green grow around the edges of the stones, and the brass still has the polish of newness. The file for the image is titled "Stolpersteine_Köln,_Markus_Meyer_(Mauritiussteinweg_81). jpg." I return to the search engine, this time typing "Mauritiussteinweg 81" and "Köln." I know it must be an address.

The internet gives me a view from the street of a beige apartment building at a shadowy time of the day. Thick vines crawl up the façade. There are blotches of blue graffiti below the windows on the first floor. Out front, cars are parked with only centimeters between the bumpers. The effect of the scene is so modern; I can't imagine Markus stepping onto this same sidewalk, perhaps hurrying toward his butcher shop nearby. He was, my father says, the kind of Jew who didn't identify as a Jew "until Hitler made him think of himself as Jewish." I don't have a photograph of his face and can't reconstruct him like one of Shimon Attie's projections of light. Here, let me try to make his image come alive: he is walking in his wool jacket on a Saturday morning, his head topped with a fedora or else bare, a newspaper tucked under his arm.

No, it doesn't work. Markus lived in a different Köln. He survived the hyperinflation of the Great Depression, carrying suitcases of money to buy goods—millions of marks for a loaf of bread—and then, as my father tells me, "did well and ended up wealthy." The leap between that Köln and the one on my computer screen is too large to take.

This last time, after nearly five months of searching, I type Markus's information—surname and first, year of birth—in the online database of the United States Holocaust Memorial Museum. There are four results, including one for a document titled "List of deaths reported on May 22nd, 1942." According to the site, fifty-one Jews were reported dead on that day. I can request a scanned copy of the text, which is described as "moderately legible."

Within minutes, the Museum has emailed the digital document. Kliger. Lindt. Braun. I run my finger down the length of my computer screen, following the list of handwritten names, many difficult to make out. The page was scanned at a slant, so that the columns lean sidewise as if with dizziness. Markus Meyer is number 38 on the page, his address a smudge. And what I hoped to find—a cause of death—is simply not there.

In Jonathan Safran Foer's novel *Everything Is Illuminated*, the narrator asserts that Jews have six senses: touch, taste, sight, smell, hearing, and memory. "[M]emory," Foer writes, "is no less primary than the prick of a pin, or its silver glimmer, or the taste of the blood it pulls from the finger. The Jew is pricked by a pin and remembers other pins. It is only by tracing the pinprick back to other pinpricks . . . that the Jew is able to know why it hurts."

But there is little inside me that is pierced by the name Markus Meyer. And my father can't remember before me. And my grandmother, who might have told me about the sound of Markus's voice or how he drank his coffee or which were his favorite lieder by Schubert, has been dead nearly four decades.

I can only make a story out of absence. The mind lurches toward different endings—I can say Markus Meyer, a man who before the war was a successful butcher in Köln, finally ran out of food and money in the ghetto. He starved. Or I can make a story of the room where he lived with Theresia in a crowded building on a street in the Łódź ghetto called Hohensteiner. No heat or medicine. No clean water. I can say it was one of the many diseases that killed him, tuberculosis or dysentery, diphtheria.

I may never know how Markus died. My inability to find the details of his death angers me, as when I have failed to find an ending for one of my poems, the lines of language left unfinished, an image so heavy it cannot flutter its wings to lift into the air. And, yes, I know this analogy transgresses.

But more than my own failure at narrative, the pinprick of Markus's memory hurts because I barely feel it. There is no point of blood at the tip of my finger. If I hold my hands out in front of me, I see the lifelines clear and deep across my palms, the legibility only of my skin.

და

When I first began studying the Shoah as a young graduate student, all the texts I am now hardened to made me cry. It would be impossible to keep reading, I knew, if every description of a railcar made me want to rub my face in ash, tear my own sleeve, cover the mirrors in my house, with every page sitting shiva over and over again for the innumerable dead and for those in my family, the ancestors I would never find, their names not handed down, their grave markers overturned or ground to sand, no pebbles left to remember, and even the ground erased of them.

If I wanted to study the Shoah, then I needed to become less porous.

And yet, the stumbling stone. After I see the picture of my great-grandfather's Stolperstein on the small field of my computer screen, I feel my body go both cold and hot. The hairs on my arms prickle. There is a sudden gravel in my throat.

Two days ago, a friend—knowing I was writing this essay—sent me an article written by a daughter of Holocaust survivors. The author, Helen Epstein, had three Stolpersteine placed in Prague to honor her mother and two of her grandparents. "How to remember," Epstein asks, "victims of mass murder who have no graves? For families whose members have survived genocide or other forms of mass murder, remembrance is private and visceral."

I don't know who commissioned Markus's stone. Maybe it was my third cousin, gone silent again, my last email never answered. Maybe it was another name on the family tree she sent me, a stranger alive in a distant part of the world. There is so much of the story that will not be resolved. They are breadcrumbs my hands cannot find in a fairytale forest, and the birds go on making their throttled songs.

And then, on the seventy-fifth anniversary of the liberation of Auschwitz, as I am preparing to teach Anna Rabinowitz's book-length Holocaust poem *Darkling*, I come across this moment: "And it's so hard to find the stepping stones. // Elsewhere is a long way away." Near the end of *Darkling*, Rabinowitz writes, "you must stumble // you must stumble // these stumbling blocks in your hands." Confluences. Everything converging. But even in these places of intersection, the gaps remain.

It's time I decided whether to keep blundering into those absences or to step over them.

Earlier, I wrote of Markus Meyer that the memory of him "hurts because I barely feel it." It's true. He doesn't draw blood in me. The pain is the duller kind. I stub my toe against the not knowing of what happened to him. He is there in the bruise on my foot, the small twinge of choosing perhaps to walk away.

Still Life with Tattered Passport

My childhood was a painting in the Flemish fashion, objects arranged on a velvet cloth, and the chiaroscuro of the scene. Consider the black booklet, its pages stamped in red. Consider the bowl of mushrooms from the woods. The poppies, drooping-necked. And all of it allegorical—that the slumped carp on the table meant something was always dying, a place or politics, a language I left behind. That the lump of amber meant I kept washing ashore. That memory was an insect fixed inside a golden fragment of the sea.

GALLERY SIX

About the Artist

The needle is the length of my pointer finger. It's cut from a piece of purpleheart, a wood that when freshly hewn is the color of an amethyst. Purpleheart darkens with age and exposure, first to the shade of eggplant skin and later to a purple tinged brown like a bruise.

Of the many small objects in my house, I love the purple needle most of all. My husband carved it for me more than two decades ago, along with a set of straight pins made from slivers of ebony, maple, and walnut. Each one is sharp but delicate. They are imperfect, slightly asymmetrical, as things made by hand often are.

The purpleheart needle isn't intended for sewing. It's entirely decorative, its point too thick to pierce cloth or to nudge a splinter from a finger. All it does is sit on a bookshelf. Occasionally, I pick it up, squint through its eye to see a sliver of the room beyond: the bed, the lamp, the tufted edge of a woven carpet. The needle's eye is like a magnifying lens in miniature; it focuses my vision, helps me to see each object more clearly.

Even when I don't look through the eye of the purpleheart needle, I scan the space around me, assessing color and balance and the shape of a line. I judge the placement of one object in relation to another, this chair beside this table, this vase beside this bowl. My gaze makes these judgments as if by instinct. "Discern," from Old French, meaning to separate by sifting, as if sight is like a sieve that separates the lumps from the fine particles.

When I was a child in Warsaw, my parents often took me on cold afternoons to visit the studios of artists. I liked to move along the edges of the rooms, to stand alone in the radiant environment of each canvas. I looked by myself. While my parents talked to the artist, the swishing sound of Polish behind me, I crossed the wood floors, feeling the low creak against my shoes, the floorboards rough, splattered with oils, acrylics, drops of adhesive.

In my memory, the artist was always an old man. He was thin or big-bellied. His fingers were nicotined yellow. He was sober or several vodka shots into his day. But no matter the size of his body or how slurred his speech, the artist always spoke fiercely about art, the way others might speak about religion or politics.

"What it means to create," he might have said, pointing the neon tip of a lighted cigarette at something half-finished on an easel. He would have nodded then, as if in agreement with himself.

I didn't take off my coat or mittens. The rooms were always cold, coal dust on every interior surface and winter coming in through the single-paned windows. The artist leaned against a doorjamb in his rolled-up shirtsleeves, so warm with making that he didn't notice the small cloud his breath left in the frigid air before him. All he saw was the pale snow of the canvases gradually overtaken by color.

On these expeditions, I was my parents' consultant, perhaps twelve or thirteen at the time. It was my duty, I understood, to help my mother and father choose well.

"No, this one," I said, leading them over to whichever painting I saw was the best.

I preferred the pieces that leaned in dark corners, the ones partly visible, stacked behind other paintings, left there as if forgotten or else waiting to be seen.

And if the artist asked why a certain piece was my favorite, I answered, "Because of the red right here." I said, "Because of the movement of this brushstroke."

An artist was once so startled by my verdicts of *yes* and *no* that he gave me a small blue oil painting. "The way she sees," he told my parents. "It is—." He gestured in the air with the nub of his cigarette, as if trying to singe the word for how I saw.

The painting still hangs on my wall. *Paysage*, the artist wrote in the bottom left corner—landscape, although the whole thing is blue, blue layered on blue, the horizon demarcated with a squiggle of white. I often misread the title of the piece, not *Paysage* but *Passage*, as in the narrow way, my vision precise, slender as the eye of a needle.

Acknowledgments

The following essays in this collection were previously published, sometimes in slightly different form:

Alaska Quarterly Review—"Ambivalent Things"
Bat City Review—"Snapshots / Denton, 2018" published as "Divided Cities"
Cincinnati Review—"Seventy-Seven Steps"
Colorado Review—"Portrait on Metal with Patterned Scarf and Streak of Light" and "Provenance"
The Common—"The Red Picture and the Blue"
Image Journal—"The Dead Class"
Massachusetts Review—"Mother and Child"
New England Review—"Essay, Made of Antique Glass"
The Normal School—"On the Color Matching System; Or, Marriage"
River Teeth—"Snapshot / Washington, DC, 1986" published as "Brood"
Seneca Review—"From the Archives: Lessons in American English"
Southeast Review—"Snapshot / Warsaw, 1981" published as "Martial Law"
West Branch—"You Must Stumble"

☙

"Portrait on Metal with Patterned Scarf and Streak of Light" listed as Notable Essay in *Best American Essays*, edited by André Aciman (Mariner Books, 2020).
"Snapshot / Lubumbashi, 1978" published as "Photograph of My Mother" in *Bound*, edited by Nayt Rundquist (New Rivers Press, 2022).

☙

Enormous gratitude to the writers, editors, and mentors who helped to shape the essays in this collection: Jennifer Acker, Harrison Candelaria Fletcher, Jill Christman, Stephanie G'Schwind, James Allen Hall, Carolyn Kuebler, Patrick Madden, Yerra Sugarman, Julie Marie Wade, Juliet Way-Henthorne, and Lauren Winner.

Works Cited

THE RED PICTURE AND THE BLUE

Abadžić Hodžić, Aida. "Mersad Berber: An Opulent Allegory of Bosnia." In *Mersad Berber: An Allegory of Bosnia*, n.p. Beyoglu: Pera Museum, 2017. Exhibition catalogue.

Doder, Dusko. "Yugoslavia: New War, Old Hatreds." *Foreign Policy*, June 19, 1993. foreignpolicy.com/1993/06/19/yugoslavia-new-war-old-hatreds.

Lucie-Smith, Edward. "Mersad Berber—A Triumphant Cultural Paradox." In *Mersad Berber: An Allegory of Bosnia*, n.p. Beyoglu: Pera Museum, 2017. Exhibition catalogue.

Plato. *Phaedrus*. Translated by W. C. Helmbold and W. G. Rabinowitz. New York: Macmillan, 1956.

Power, Samantha. *"A Problem from Hell": America and the Age of Genocide.* New York: Basic Books, 2002.

United Nations. "International Criminal Tribunal for the Former Yugoslavia: The Conflicts." United Nations International Residual Mechanism for Criminal Tribunals. www.icty.org/en/about/what-former-yugoslavia/conflicts.

THE DEAD CLASS

Gussow, Mel. "Tadeusz Kantor's Troupe Carries On." *New York Times*, June 14, 1991. http://www.nytimes.com/1991/06/14/theater/review-theater-tadeusz-kantor-s-troupe-carries-on.html.

Kantor, Tadeusz. *The Dead Class.* Directed by Andrzej Wajda. Performed by Tadeusz Kantor and Cricot 2. Telewizja Polska, 1976. YouTube. www.youtube.com/watch?v=a235hHGFIps.

———. *A Journey through Other Spaces: Essays and Manifestos, 1944–1990.* Translated by Michał Kobiałka. Berkeley: University of California Press, 1993.

Kobiałka, Michał. "A Requiem for Tadeusz Kantor." *PAJ: A Journal of Performance and Art* 38, no. 3 (2016): 3-18.

Pinsky, Robert. *The Figured Wheel.* New York: Farrar, Strauss and Giroux, 1996.

"Poland's President Supports Making Some Holocaust Statements a Crime." *New York Times*, February 6, 2018. www.nytimes.com/2018/02/06/world/europe/poland-holocaust-law.html?module=inline.

Romanska, Magda. Interview with Anthem Press. Originally published on the Anthem Press Blog, May 9, 2014. magdaromanska.com/interview-with-magda-romanska-author-of-the-post-traumatic-theatre-of-grotowski-and-kantor-2/.

"Tadeusz Kantor, 75, Polish Theater Director." *New York Times*, May 5, 2017. www.nytimes.com/1990/12/09/obituaries/tadeusz-kantor-75polish-theater-director.html.

Witts, Noel. *Tadeusz Kantor*. London: Routledge, 2010.

ESSAY, MADE OF ANTIQUE GLASS

Baudelaire, Charles. "Poor Belgium: The Argument." Translated by Richard Sieburth. *Conjunctions* 62 (2014): 125–45.

The Bible. Authorized King James Version. Oxford: Oxford World Classics, 2008.

Conrad, Joseph. *Heart of Darkness*. New York: Dover, 1990.

Des Forges, Alison. *"Leave None to Tell the Story": Genocide in Rwanda*. Human Rights Watch. March 1, 1999. www.hrw.org/reports/1999/rwanda/.

Gontar, Cybele. "Art Nouveau." Metropolitan Museum of Art. Heilbrunn Timeline of Art History. October 2006. www.metmuseum.org/toah/hd/artn/hd_artn.html.

Gourevitch, Philip. *We Wish to Inform You That Tomorrow We Will Be Killed with Our Families*. London: Picador, 1998.

Landler, Mark. "Declassified U.N. Cables Reveal Turning Point in Rwanda Crisis of 1994." *New York Times*, June 3, 2014. www.nytimes.com/2014/06/04/world/africa/un-cables-reveal-a-turning-point-in-rwanda-crisis.html.

Mannoni, Edith. *Schneider*. Translated by Mary Scott. Paris: Massin, 1992.

"Rwanda Monitoring Group." National Security Archive. nsarchive2.gwu.edu/NSAEBB/NSAEBB500/docs/Document 08.pdf.

Silverman, Debora L. "Art Nouveau, Art of Darkness: African Lineages of Belgian Modernism, Part 1." *West 86th: A Journal of Decorative Arts, Design History, and Material Culture* 19, no. 2 (2012): 175–95.

PORTRAIT ON METAL WITH
PATTERNED SCARF AND STREAK OF LIGHT

Barthes, Roland. *Camera Lucida: Reflections on Photography*. Translated by Richard Howard. New York: Farrar, Strauss and Giroux, 1981.

Freud, Sigmund. *The Interpretation of Dreams*. Translated by James Strachey. New York: Avon Books, 1965.

Sontag, Susan. *On Photography*. New York: Farrar, Strauss and Giroux, 1977.

LOST VESSELS

"Before the North Carolina Medical Board." Health Grades. healthgrades.com/media/english/pdf/sanctions/HGPYYMGR208112020.pdf.

Dafoe, Taylor. "The Smithsonian Institution Is Rebranding Its Arthur M. Sackler Gallery in Washington." *Art World*, December 5, 2019. news.artnet.com/art-world/sackler-gallery-rebrand-1723587.

Doty, Mark. "Bride in Beige." In *Truth in Nonfiction*, edited by David Lazar, 11–16. Iowa City: University of Iowa Press, 2008.

Fowler, Hayley. "NC Doctor Fed Florida Man's Opioid Addiction Until It Killed Him, Prosecutor Says." *Charlotte Observer*, December 18, 2019. charlotteobserver.com/news/state/north-carolina/article238518828.html.

Keefe, Patrick Radden. "The Family That Built an Empire of Pain." *New Yorker*, October 23, 2017. newyorker.com/magazine/2017/10/30/the-family-that-built-an-empire-of-pain.

Merkley, Jeffrey A. Letter to Lonnie G. Bunch III. June 19, 2019. Jeff Merkley: United States Senator for Oregon. merkley.senate.gov/imo/media/doc/19.06.19 LTR Merkley to Smithsonian_Sackler Gallery.pdf.

National Museum of Asian Art. "About the Arthur M. Sackler Gallery." asia.si.edu/about/about-the-arthur-m-sackler-gallery/.

———. "Opium Pipe Bowl." asia.si.edu/object/S2012.9.3945/.

"Patient Information for SUBOXONE." Suboxone. www.suboxone.com.

US Attorney's Office, Middle District of North Carolina. "Rowan County Doctor Sentenced for Unlawful Distribution of Prescription Opioids." December 17, 2019. justice.gov/usao-mdnc/pr/rowan-county-doctor-sentenced-unlawful-distribution-prescription-opioids.

US Food and Drug Administration. "Medication Guide, OxyContin." fda.gov/media/78453/download.

Zee, Art Van. "The Promotion and Marketing of OxyContin: Commercial Triumph, Public Health Tragedy." *American Journal of Public Health*, February 2009. ncbi.nlm.nih.gov/pmc/articles/PMC2622774/.

SEVENTY-SEVEN STEPS

Bernstein, Jacob. "Jens Risom, Modernist Designer Whose Furniture Still Has Legs, Dies at 100." *New York Times*, December 22, 2016. www.nytimes.com/2016/12/22/world/europe/jens-risom-dead.html.

Demetrios, Eames. *An Eames Primer.* New York: Universe Publishing, 2001.

Demetrios, Eames, dir. *77 Steps.* Vimeo. May 21, 2012. vimeo.com/42591587.

"Dependent." Online Etymology Dictionary. www.etymonline.com/word/ dependent.

Emeco. "Corporate Background." Press Kit. www.emeco.net/press.

THE LODGER

Dubrow, Jehanne. *throughsmoke: an essay in notes.* Moorehead, MN: New Rivers Press, 2019.

"lodge, n." *Oxford English Dictionary.*

Sartwell, Crispin. *Six Names of Beauty.* London: Routledge, 2006.

Scarry, Elaine. *On Beauty and Being Just.* Princeton, NJ: Princeton University Press, 1999.

Scruton, Roger. *Beauty: A Very Short Introduction.* Oxford: Oxford University Press, 2011.

Stendahl. *Rome, Naples, and Florence.* Translated by Richard N. Coe. London: John Calder, 2010.

AMBIVALENT THINGS

The Bible. King James Version. www.biblegateway.com/passage/?search=Genesis+22&version=KJV.

Brown, Bill. "Thing Theory." *Critical Inquiry* 28, no. 1 (2001): 1–22.

Mendelsohn, Daniel. *The Lost: A Search for Six of Six Million.* New York: Harper, 2013.

"Stigma." Online Etymology Dictionary. www.etymonline.com/word/stigma.

DEAR ROSE

Brettel, Rick. "'Dior' at the Dallas Museum of Art Is a Jaw-Dropping Fashion Art Exhibition." *Dallas Morning News*, May 16, 2019. www.dallasnews.com/ arts-entertainment/architecture/2019/05/16/dior-at-the-dallas-museum-of-art-is-a-jaw-dropping-fashion-art-exhibition.

Dior: From Paris to the World. Dallas: Dallas Museum of Art, 2019. Exhibition catalogue.

Horyn, Cathy. "Galliano Case Tests Dior Brand's Future." *New York Times*, March 1, 2011. www.nytimes.com/2011/03/02/fashion/02galliano-dior.html.

Pinsky, Robert. *The Figured Wheel: New and Collected Poems 1966–1996.* New York: Farrar, Strauss and Giroux, 1996.

PROVENANCE

Eliot, George. *Daniel Deronda*. London: Penguin Classics, 1996.

O'Connor, Anne-Marie. *The Lady in Gold: The Extraordinary Tale of Gustav Klimt's Masterpiece, "Portrait of Adele Bloch-Bauer."* New York: Vintage, 2015.

Prinz, Deborah R. "Celebrating the Sacher Torte." *Forward*, December 5, 2015. forward.com/food/326015/celebrating-the-sacher-torte.

United States Holocaust Memorial Museum. "Austria." Holocaust Encyclopedia. encyclopedia.ushmm.org/content/en/article/austria.

Vogel, Carol. "Lauder Pays $135 Million, a Record, for a Klimt Portrait." *New York Times*, June 19, 2006. www.nytimes.com/2006/06/19/arts/design/19klim.html.

THE RESONATOR

Celan, Paul. *Selected Poems and Prose of Paul Celan*. Translated by John Felstiner. New York: W. W. Norton, 2001.

Cohen, Jeffrey Jerome. "Feeling Stone." *SubStance* 47, no. 2 (2018): 23–35.

Freed, James Ingo. "The United States Holocaust Memorial Museum." *Assemblage* 41, no. 9 (1989): 58–79.

Linenthal, Edward T. *Preserving Memory: The Struggle to Create America's Holocaust Museum*. New York: Columbia University Press, 2001.

Romaine, James. "Gravity and Grace: The Art of Richard Serra." *Image* 57. image-journal.org/article/gravity-and-grace.

United States Holocaust Memorial Museum. "About the Museum: Architecture and Art." www.ushmm.org/information/about-the-museum/architecture-and-art.

Wiesel, Eli. "Art and the Holocaust: Trivializing Memory." *New York Times*, June 11, 1989. www.nytimes.com/1989/06/11/movies/art-and-the-holocaust-trivializing-memory.html.

YOU MUST STUMBLE

Aligheri, Dante. *The Inferno*. Translated by Robert Hollander and Jean Hollander. New York: Anchor Books, 2002.

Budnitz, Judy. "Hershel." In *Lost Tribe: Jewish Fiction from the Edge*, edited by Paul Zakrzewski, 183–91. New York: Perennial, 2003.

Demnig, Gunter. "Stolpersteine." www.stolpersteine.eu/en/home/. Accessed January 10, 2019.

Epstein, Helen. "How Do We Remember Victims of Mass Murder? A Holocaust

Survivor's Daughter on How She Honors Her Family." *Time*, January 24, 2020. time.com/5771188/remember-victims-holocaust-survivors-daughter/.

Foer, Jonathan Safran. *Everything Is Illuminated*. New York: Perennial, 2003.

Grieshaber, Kirsten. "Plaques for Nazi Victims Offer a Personal Impact." *New York Times*, November 29, 2003. www.nytimes.com/2003/11/29/arts/plaques-for-nazi-victims-offer-a-personal-impact.html.

Hecht, Anthony. *Collected Later Poems*. New York: Knopf, 2005.

Kluth, Andreas. "Stumbling Over the Past." *1843 Magazine*, May/June 2013.

Rabinowitz, Anna. *Darkling*. Dorset, VT: Tupelo, 2001.

United States Holocaust Memorial Museum. Holocaust Encyclopedia. encyclopedia.ushmm.org.

Young, James. *At Memory's Edge: After-Images of the Holocaust in Contemporary Art and Architecture*. New Haven, CT: Yale University Press, 2000.